# Diversity, Equity, and Inclusion

## Strategies for Facilitating Conversations on Race

# Diversity, Equity, and Inclusion

## Strategies for Facilitating Conversations on Race

Caprice D. Hollins
Ilsa M. Govan

ROWMAN & LITTLEFIELD
Lanham • Boulder • New York • London

Published by Rowman & Littlefield
A wholly owned subsidiary of The Rowman & Littlefield Publishing Group, Inc.
4501 Forbes Boulevard, Suite 200, Lanham, Maryland 20706
www.rowman.com

Unit A, Whiteacre Mews, 26-34 Stannary Street, London SE11 4AB

British Library Cataloguing in Publication Information Available

**Library of Congress Cataloging-in-Publication Data**

Hollins, Caprice D.
  Diversity, equity, and inclusion : strategies for facilitating conversations on race / Caprice D. Hollins, Ilsa M. Govan.
      pages cm
  Includes bibliographical references.
  ISBN 978-1-4758-1498-9 (pbk.) — ISBN 978-1-4758-1499-6 (e-book)  1. Group facilitation. 2. Intercultural communication. 3. Race relations. 4. Racism. I. Govan, Ilsa M. II. Title.
  HM751.H65 2015
  305.8—dc23
                                   2014043862

Printed in the United States of America

Caprice Hollins:

This book is dedicated to my husband, who has supported me in countless ways so that I could live my dream, and to my children, Matae and Makena, who love me unconditionally, bring balance to my life, and always remind me that social justice begins at home.

Ilsa M. Govan:

This book is dedicated to all of the organizers, educators, facilitators, and community members engaged in the daily work for social and environmental justice.

# Contents

# Preface

My mom, Darlene Jones, is white, and my dad, Sam Jones, is black. I have four older brothers and sisters, Mike, Ted, Kelly, and Mark, who are all white, with blond hair and blue eyes, from my mom's first marriage, and a younger sister, Suzanne, who is also multiracial. My mother was born and raised in Washington, grew up Catholic and married at the age of 18, shortly after becoming pregnant with her first child. She ultimately ended up divorcing her husband and, three years after her fourth child was born, became pregnant with me. This created a strain on her relationship with her parents. A white woman, on welfare raising six children alone, two of whom were mixed race, during the 1960s was something that most people disapproved of, to say the least.

She met my grandparents, Marion and George Simmons, a black couple who didn't have children of their own, while pregnant with me. She started working for them in their barbecue restaurant and catering business. Eventually she started calling them "Mama" and "Papa" and we kids called them "Grandma" and "Grandpa." After our sister Kelly died from viral encephalitis at the age of 14, my mother started working intermittently on the Alaskan pipeline, and she volunteered as a firefighter. Mark, Suzanne, and I went to live with our grandparents during these times. A few years later my mother and grandparents realized that if something was to happen to her we could be dispersed by the state, so they legally adopted her when she was 42 years old. I also grew up with two older African-American foster siblings, Robert and Judy Wilkins, who stayed with us when things got tough in their home.

My brother Mark was openly gay at an early age. My aunts and uncles are my mother's best friends, and my cousins are their children. I have always relished the diversity in my family, but it wasn't until graduate school that I began to understand and acknowledge how I unconsciously stereotyped people in harmful ways because of their differences.

My area of focus in graduate school was clinical psychology, with an emphasis in multicultural and community psychology. We spent the entire first year unpacking our bias and exploring the dynamics of difference. Because my family was so diverse, I thought I didn't hold any stereotypes, prejudices, or negative attitudes towards people who were different from me, certainly not racial difference, after all, my mom is white! My diverse family experiences became proof of my truth that I was free from bias and stereotyping, making it more challenging for me to explore ways in which I had benefited from privileges as a multiracial, light-skinned woman. It didn't take long for me to begin to see that my attitudes and beliefs were deeply engrained in my psyche—not only about people who were different from me, but also towards those groups with whom I identified. It was a tender time in my life that involved a lot of pain, anger, shame, guilt, and, sometimes, denial. But the freedom I gained from embracing all of who I am and the ways in which it has deepened my relationships with others has been well worth the journey.

I often see my old ways of being and thinking reflected in the words and actions of people I now work with as I help navigate them through their journey of open, honest, and critical reflection around race relations, and I get excited for them and the possibilities of who we can become. I understand that this work is demanding, complicated, and exhausting, but I also know that there is no better feeling than to see yourself and the world as they really are. When you have an awakening, the dance of discomfort in cross-cultural relationships begins to dissipate. You begin to shake the fear of truly being seen, and you learn to embrace not only your strengths but your humanness. Somehow along the way you learn to love yourself better, and with this evolve a freedom and inner peace that can lead you on a course of action and advocacy towards social justice. This is why I love this work. Because while it is difficult beyond words, it is also rewarding beyond measure—it is our hope for a better tomorrow.

# WHERE I'M FROM

Caprice Hollins—7/17/08

I'm from an Irish and Scottish world; translated—white, who never fully accepted me but never quite rejected me, like the way they did my dark skinned sisters. I'm from African Queens who take pride in the gaps between their teeth, until years of enslavement divided us with "You think you're better than me don't you?"

*That's where I'm from*

I'm from a laid back, pool-playing absent father who had children I've never met and "Your daddy loves you honey, he's a good man." I'm from a pimp for a step dad, Lester Lee Wingate the III, but there were still fun times, in Ketchikan and Valdez, and hey, we got a new baby sister now.

*That's where I'm from*

I'm from a mother who made us a family when her own turned the other way, who loved me with all her being, who believed that I was beautiful, whose eyes would beam with pride at every step I took, who would take away all my pain if she could, "You have the world to fight, don't fight one another," shot gun in her hand if anyone was to ever try to hurt one of her babies, and "Don't judge one another," kind of mother.

*That's where I'm from*

I'm from Marion and George's barbecue and catering on 23rd and Judkins, grandparents who found the blessing of being grandparents in me, piled high on their bed watching old black and whites seeing whites dressed as Chinese and Indians? Playing penny ante poker, homemade potato chips, costumes, jams and jellies, and a kitchen that always smelled ooh sooo good—everything from scratch except for the closet full of toilet paper and paper towels, because you just never know, and "How come you don't have more black friends honey?"

*That's where I'm from*

I'm from Myrtle Creek Oregon, white grandparents who were ashamed of the color of my skin; hearing taunts of "Nigger go home!" where teachers pretended they didn't hear, and a white grandmother who believed if she told me to just ignore it that I actually could. Can't wait to go home because names do hurt me.

I'm from Gumbo, Oxtail Stew, Collard Greens, Mahalia Jackson on clean up Sundays, Michael Jackson's *Enjoy Yourself,* steppin' to the groove and doin' the bump, if you can.

I'm from summer trips to the Oregon Coast, to visit Father Timmy and Uncle Billy and "Mommy, who's Jim Crow?" *Whistle while you work, Nixon is a...* "You kids knock that off!"

*That's where I'm from*

I'm from Coupeville Washington, loving summer life on the farm until... "What's that you're putting in your hair?" and "You must be good at basketball." I don't need to ask you why you won't ask me to dance, I already know, because you nicknamed me Shadow and played games called Nigger Knocking, then said you were sorry that you wanted to invite me to your sleepover but couldn't.

I'm from a family who loves me but a world that still judges me, because of the color of my skin.

*Where are you from?*

My sister and I were talking about racism the other day, and she asked if constantly trying the see the world from multiple perspectives and take into account personal, cultural, and systemic privilege with folks wasn't exhausting. Why would anyone choose to think about these things? Perhaps, she suggested, it is because of some awkward struggles I had with my own self-esteem growing up that I cling so passionately to my current identity as an antiracist white person.

These are the kinds of questions I hear frequently. Why would any white person choose to see the world in a way that so clearly illustrates our responsibility for ending racism? How can it be in our best interest to see ourselves as a part of a group that obviously participated/participates in the disadvantaging, even genocide of others?

I believe my sister inadvertently played a role in my becoming a social justice activist. Growing up with a sibling less than two years younger made me acutely aware of what is and is not fair from a very early age. My parents catered to our desire for equity by setting up rules, such as those regarding splitting the rare bottle of Coke. One of us got to pour the soda into two glasses; the other got to choose the first glass.

Their concerns, however, were not limited to food-and-drink justice. I attended my first Take Back the Night march when I was in first grade. In third grade, I was shocked and outraged when one of my parents' friends was killed in a hate crime because he was gay. By the time I reached college, I was familiar with racial bias in textbooks, sexism in Disney movies, and homophobia in the churches many of my peers attended. The next logical step was an awareness of the everyday manifestations of white privilege in my life. I was primed for taking on the many injustices of the world.

At first, advocating for justice was about my own rights. As a child, I complained when adults talked down to me and didn't take my opinions and values seriously. I worked hard to define myself as a woman free of the social constructions of beauty and gender roles that limited my full expression. I learned to spit. When really exploring white privilege in college, I sought out ways that I could use my privilege to benefit others. My idea of justice for all involved speaking up for others and advocating so they would not be mistreated.

Further exploration of social and environmental justice has led me to believe that advocating for equity serves all people. We have all been put into politically constructed boxes that not only limit our self-expression but also separate us from one another. Thus, my personal and professional relationships are inhibited by systematic segregation. In addition, institutional racism in our society weighs heavily on my soul. My morality depends on first acknowledging and then breaking down the walls of these boxes. How is it fair to any of us to live in a world where we are taught lies and half-truths about each other?

With the complexities of racism, there is no clear path to bridging the divisions I learned, despite my parents' best intentions. But the true joy of advocating for justice lies not only in the result but also in the process. There is a rush of energy I feel with new learning and connections to others—the "runner's high" of social justice work that comes from sticking with it despite the obstacles. Living with integrity and purposefully seeking understanding of others and my own self will never be exhausting. In fact, it is exhilarating.

## WHERE I'M FROM

Ilsa Govan

I am from the top knuckle on the ring finger of Michigan.
Born of parents who knew what they did not want to be—
Catholic, abusive, war supporters, White collar American business people—
And sought new ways to define community.

I am from European Americans
Gauvins, Skomskis, Ursas and Guenthers
Who gave up our names, language and culture to be White Americans,
Then look to others to replace our loss.
Spiritual samplers dancing between appropriation and appreciation.
My favorite color is rainbow, my best friend is black, and love sees no color.

I am from the School of Light And Realization,
Communal living where I practiced flying,
Dug holes to China,
Said Oms before dinner
And my imaginary friends were named She-He and Power.

I am from organic vegetables picked fresh from the garden for dinner
And games of euchre on icy midwest evenings.
Hot baths with my sister singing,
"Looking for a heart headed woman,"
As we wrap our heads in hearts of bubbles.

I am from branches so thin they almost break
As the wind blows me back and forth
And mom says, "As long as you can get yourself down you can climb up."

I am from a feminist mother,
Marching to Take Back the Night
And explaining to the kids in the neighborhood
What Prince meant when he saw Nikki
"Masturbating with a magazine."
"I'm sorry, my girls don't talk baby talk."
Sunday cleaning to the oldies
Because no matter how poor you are,
Your house should always be clean.
And yes, mama did take acid.

I am from a dad who cries at Hallmark commercials
And cried when he heard this poem.
Who played guitar and sang songs for his two girls.
"I like me, I'm as happy as can be ..."

I am from parents twice married and twice divorced,
To and from each other.

I am from thunderstorms,
Water rushing around me
As I sit at the end of the apartment parking lot
And make boats out of sticks and leaves.
I am from Joey Brown, the 1976 Mercury Marquis,
Who liked to honk his own horn.
Crouched down in the backseat,
Hoping nobody sees me.

I am from failed attempts at popularity
I didn't have Guess Jeans or the Country Club code
And couldn't figure out why just being myself
Was never enough.

I am from a family
1000s of miles from other relatives,
Looking for something new, better, redefinition.

I am from nights that end with Huggabuggaboo, a kiss, and I love you.

   That's where I'm from.

# Introduction

Above all, the facilitator should have a good understanding of racism. This includes both an awareness on a personal level of your own prejudices and assumptions and an ability to analyze and describe racism on an institutional and cultural level.

—Judith Katz

We have been facilitating conversations on race for about 30 years collectively, but it wasn't until working together in a large urban school district that we both took on the role of designing curriculum for training trainers. At that time we were training principals, teachers, paraprofessionals, nurses, administrative assistants, and anyone else in our district who was interested in being a part of an Equity Team. The majority of those we trained had little or no prior experience facilitating workshops on race. The only qualifications they needed were the desire to lead, the willingness to learn, and some level of awareness around their own socialization as racial beings.

We got the idea to bring *Diversity, Equity, and Inclusion: Strategies for Facilitating Conversations on Race* to our surrounding community when we attended a race relations workshop together. We noticed that these experienced and well-respected facilitators avoided navigating participants through difficult and awkward issues that came up during the activities. When tension became evident, the facilitators either called for a moment of silence or moved on to the next part of the exercise. It was clear to us that they struggled with how to help participants go deeper into the work. They had their agenda planned full of engaging effective activities but struggled with what to do when participants took them off course. This experience created in us a desire to help facilitators become more skilled at navigating courageous conversations. As a result we decided to design a training that addressed our most common experiences as facilitators and strategies that we found helpful in moving participants through the tension. We wanted to capture challenges we face as facilitators—the unexpected comments and group dynamics that can take you by surprise but are seldom written out in activity instructions.

Together, we developed a full-day workshop to help new and seasoned facilitators engage participants in courageous conversations. The response was overwhelmingly positive. Participants included firefighters, school district administrators, church leaders, teachers, childcare providers, government employees, community advocates, and a host of other people from varying backgrounds, positions, and experiences. It was then we realized the need to write a book that would make this information accessible to a larger audience. We have written *Diver-*

*sity, Equity, and Inclusion* for those who are interested in taking on a transformative leadership role within their organization. It is our intent to better equip facilitators with the necessary tools and strategies for dealing with stumbling blocks that often arise when people are brought together to talk about some of the most difficult issues facing our country today—racism, power, and privilege.

This book is designed for those who are first-time facilitators and for the more experienced who want to improve their facilitation skills. Keep in mind, it is not designed to further your self-awareness or knowledge of the social and political constructs of oppression and privilege. That work is a necessary prerequisite for becoming a facilitator, and it is critical that you have begun your own personal journey towards cultural competences before attempting to facilitate others on theirs. As Parker Palmer says, "Good leadership comes from people who have penetrated their own inner darkness and arrived at the place where we are at one with one another, people who can lead the rest of us to a place of 'hidden wholeness' because they have been there and know the way." We make the assumption that our readers have started and continue the process of self-awareness, which is fundamental to effective facilitation. In doing your own self-work, we also assume that you are familiar with the language we use (white privilege, power, oppression, racism, etc.). We've included a list of common terminology in the appendix. It is not logical to assume that you can facilitate another through deep exploration of race relations when you are not engaged in the process yourself.

One part of our own recent growth has been in furthering our understanding of gender identity. In this book, you may notice we frequently use "they" as a singular pronoun rather than "he/she." This is an intentional decision to acknowledge the multiple forms of gender that do not fit into the he/she binary. Unfortunately, popular rules of grammar have not caught up with people's lived experiences, and as authors contributing to that experience, we feel a responsibility to be more inclusive.

We want to recognize that becoming culturally competent is an ongoing process. This means that facilitators will continue to face new challenges they must work to overcome. Just when we think we have mastered a situation, we are met with a whole new experience we didn't expect and weren't prepared for. Sometimes we are successful in effectively navigating participants through courageous conversations, and other times we find ourselves grappling with how to proceed. We use the ineffectual moments as opportunity for growth by reflecting and discussing with each other ways in which we could have managed the situation more effectively. This approach allows us to consider every experience as a learning opportunity rather than a failure, thus preparing us for the inevitable "next time." *Diversity, Equity, and Inclusion* makes available strategies we wished we had when first starting out. While this book is not all-encompassing—after all, engaging in conversations on race is tricky business—we do hope it will aid you in successfully facilitating some of the most challenging and anxiety-provoking situations you are likely to face. As each of us takes on this difficult work to make our world a better place, we need all the help we can get. We are thankful for our allies in their willingness to take risks as we work together to transform our country so that justice is truly for all. We wish you the best on your journey.

## FOUNDATIONAL BELIEFS

In an effort to stay focused on our vision and maintain the integrity of this work, we created a list of foundational beliefs that we try to remain rooted in when engaging participants in dialogue about race.

### Our Vision

A world based on principles of equity and justice where all people recognize their roles as agents of change.

### *We believe ...*

- Oppression is taught and can be unlearned.
- Institutional racism is not our fault, but it is our responsibility to eradicate.
- People learn best when they believe they have more to learn.
- Increasing awareness of oneself is a strategy for change.
- Listening is a form of action.
- Most people are well-intentioned, even while they are unaware of how they are hurting others. Impact and outcomes matter more than intention.
- Experiencing discomfort is important to learning.
- Hurt people hurt people.
- Relationships are the foundation of cultural competence.
- Hurting, shaming, and blaming are not effective tools for opening minds and changing attitudes and assumptions.
- Building relationships across difference is not necessarily the same as confronting systems of oppression.
- Challenging racism and white privilege is everyone's work.
- Although people of color may bring a personal understanding of racism, this does not mean they fully understand the dynamics of racism, power, and privilege. Although white people may have knowledge of institutional racism and privilege, this does not mean they understand personal experiences of racism.
- It takes sustained effort to change systems. We will not naturally evolve toward greater equity.
- There are no quick fixes or cookbook approaches.
- Everyone deserves to be treated with dignity and respect.
- Change is possible. There is hope.

# SECTION I
# GETTING STARTED

The challenge of social justice is to evoke a sense of community that we need to make our nation a better place, just as we make it a safer place.

—Marian Wright Edelman

# Chapter One

## Structuring a Workshop

> It is your job to connect with your learners in a way that they will say yes when you issue the invitation to learn.
>
> —Dr. Joye Norris

*Leave plenty of time for participants to process the information.*

Developing a workshop can take quite a bit of time, particularly if it is a new workshop that you have never facilitated before. The more time you spend determining what you will cover and how you will deliver the material, the more likely your hard work will lead to a successful outcome.

Whether you are facilitating a half-day or full-day workshop, consider starting with your personal introduction, the norms and objectives for the day, then move into a warm-up activity, followed by one or two main activities, and then close with an opportunity for participants to reflect and process what they have learned from your time together. (See Appendix F, "Sample Agenda"). It is always helpful to know who your audience is and have some sense of where they are in their thinking in terms of race relations. Here are some tips to guide you in structuring a successful workshop.

### 1. Knowing Your Audience
- *Prior work.* Has your audience participated in culturally relevant professional development (CRPD) as a group or is this their first time? Oftentimes, individuals within the organization have participated in CRPD on their own but not together. Having done prior work together increases the possibility that they will be further along on the continuum of cultural competence. Find out what past work they have done as a group, what topics they covered, when they covered them, and their attitudes about it. Were they eager and open to learn about self and others, or were they resistant to change? What were the outcomes? Did they become divided, or were they able to work through any conflict or tension that had arisen? Gaining some understanding of prior learning and how they responded will give you the opportunity to develop curriculum that builds on what they've already learned and will better prepare you for what you might encounter as a facilitator. Whether they've done this work together before or not,

participants will be in different places in their understanding of race issues and in their willingness to engage in courageous conversations.

- *Attitude about the work.* How open are they to the conversation? As best as possible, try to determine the majority's attitude about CRPD. Comments like "This is a waste of my time" or "I don't see what this has to do with my work" sometimes, though not always, are indicators that they are resistant to change and therefore signify that more awareness work is needed. These types of comments cause us to pause for a moment. We wonder if they have had negative past experiences, if they truly do not understand the importance of developing their cultural competence, or if we are hearing their underlying fears talking.

- Comments like "We've done this already" or "Just tell me what I need to do" tend to come from participants who are seeking a quick fix. This is often an indicator to us that they need to do more awareness and knowledge work, not the strategies-based work they are seeking. Granted, while there are some skills that can be taught, most are developed from our awareness of self plus our knowledge of others. Skill-building strategies cannot be easily taught but, rather, are situated in context. People who have done a fair amount of this work realize this and therefore don't tend to make these types of comments because they understand that, for the most part, strategies are often practiced and developed in the moment and are heavily situated in relation to the person you are engaging.

- Awareness work is the most difficult work to engage participants in because the process of exploring your own bias, stereotypes, privilege, attitudes, beliefs, assumptions, and so on can lead to a painful awakening. It could be that participants are unconsciously resistant to having another emotionally conflicting experience.

- Gauging attitudes will help you get a sense of how open they are to having conversations about race and better prepare you to plan your workshop and respond to off-putting remarks expressed by participants. With the help of people within the organization, it will be your job to determine what they would most benefit from.

- *Racial/ethnic diversity.* What is the racial and ethnic breakdown of the participants you will be working with? Some activities are more difficult to facilitate when there is less diversity in the room. When participants of color are in the minority, it is not uncommon for them to contribute very little to the conversation. This will increase the likelihood that you will have to do more to bring the experiences of participants of color into the room in a way that does not make your participants of color a reluctant focus of attention. There are many reasons that can account for their silence. They may feel pressure and not want to represent their group's experience. They may not feel comfortable or safe enough to speak openly among their white colleagues about their true thoughts and feelings. This is often the case when their voice has been marginalized in the past. Their silence or lack of participation can also be a result of the internal work they are doing alongside their white counterparts to make meaning of what they are learning. It could also be they disagree with the perspective that race matters and they struggle to differentiate between individual experiences of racism and a collective experience of racism. How participants engage in your workshop will depend on where they are in their racial/ethnic identity development. Regardless of the reason, cultural competence is everyone's work, and so it will still be important that you engage them.

However, don't assume because you have participants of color in the room they will be able or willing to assist you in the conversation.

- When whites are in the minority, it can increase their fear that what they say may reveal their bias, prejudice, or racism. For them it may be safer to keep their thoughts and feelings to themselves rather than risk being seen in a negative way. When a white participant becomes the target of courageous conversations as a result of what they said, it is not uncommon for another white participant to say to them, "I was in your chair last time," which could mean, "I learned to keep my mouth shut or risk being in the hot seat." Personal experiences of discomfort paired with stories they have heard from friends and family can make it difficult for white participants to take risks and speak their truth.

- Having a small number of participants of color or of whites may not render your workshop ineffective, but it does present its challenges. We have found that the more diverse the participants, the more diverse the perspectives and the more engaging the conversation will be.

- *Accommodations*. Do any of the participants have a disability and need an accommodation? Will someone need an interpreter? Is anyone limited in English proficiency, or does anyone have an intellectual disability that may make reading or processing verbal information a challenge? Will your activities involving movement create a barrier for anyone? Asking these questions up front demonstrates your dedication to inclusivity and will help you prepare to make the necessary accommodations that will enable everyone to fully participate in the process.

- *Why now?* Why is the organization deciding to engage in race relations work at this time? Did something occur that brought negative public attention to their organization? Is there tension among staff? Did they become aware that they are not meeting the needs of the populations they serve? The reason they are asking you to facilitate a workshop at a particular time can greatly influence how participants feel about having these conversations. Knowing their reasons will help you to get a better picture of what they are coming into the room with, for example, fear and apprehension versus openness and interest.

- *What does the organization do?* Do I need to have the same background or experience in the organization I will be facilitating for? No. Don't misunderstand us. There is no doubt there are benefits in working with an audience with a background similar to yours. And you should gather as much information about the organization that you can in order to better understand the culture and offer up examples that are relevant to the experiences of your participants. However, having a different field of study doesn't mean you can't or shouldn't work with an organization you have little or no experience with. We have worked with many different types of organizations over the years, and more often than not we do not have experience or training in the fields of our clients. Our backgrounds in psychology and education did not render us ineffective in working with county officials or lawyers, for example. Even when we did have similar backgrounds, participants held different positions within their organization, such as administrative assistant, human resource director, accountant, custodian, and so on. You can't possibly have degrees and experience in all the different areas. What you can bring is a degree of expertise in race relations. Your goal is to help participants develop their lens and understanding, and then have them do the work to figure out how it relates to their particular function within the organization. You can do this by having them engage in discussion after an activity or lesson plan that has them explore relevancy and application, such as "How does what you learned apply to your work?"

- *Mandatory opportunity:* Sometimes people are there because they have to be. When this is the case, acknowledge it and then encourage them to be open to learning in spite of this fact.

## 2. Narrowing Your Purpose

- *Determine which of the four areas of cultural competence will be your focus*: (1) Will your workshop help them deepen their understanding of their own bias, values, beliefs, attitudes towards others?—Awareness; (2) Will it help them to develop an understanding of racially/ethnically diverse cultures?—Knowledge; (3) Will it teach them strategies for engaging across cultures?—Skills; or (4) Will it help them to institutionalize change within their organization?—Action/Advocacy. (See Table 1, and Appendix D, "What Is Cultural Competence?") Having clarity around what you want them to leave with as a result of your time together will help you build an agenda with purpose. You will likely have a limited amount of time to deliver a lot of information in a way that engages participants in deeper understanding. Don't try to do everything.

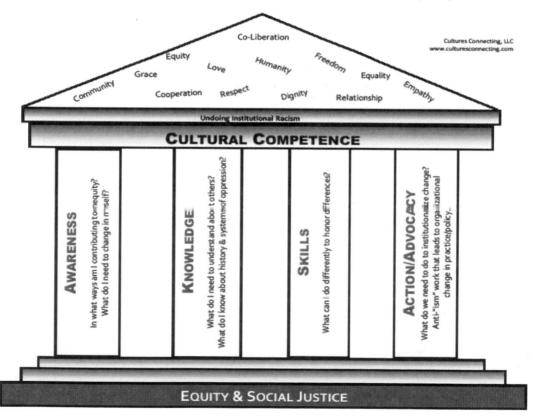

- *Decide on the objectives*. What will participants know or be able to do as a result of your time together? We recommend that you set 2 or 3 objectives for a half-day workshop and 3 to 4 objectives for a full-day workshop. You will likely discover that there is a lot that you would like to cover but not enough time to do it in. Coming up with objectives will help guide you in developing your curriculum and keep you focused on your purpose so you can accomplish what you came there to do in the limited time you have to do it in. It will also help your participants know where it is you are trying to take them and therefore alleviate confusion about the purpose of your time together. Listed below are a few examples of objectives:

- *Participants will ...*
  (1) develop insight and understanding of their own story and how it shapes their racial lens;
  (2) increase their understanding of how racial stereotypes impact learning; and
  (3) know how to identify microaggressions and understand the underlying hidden messages that increase tension across cultures.

## 3. Selecting Activities

- *Choose the right activities*. What content will you cover and what activities will best support your objectives? The next step is to come up with activities that will help you meet your objectives. Activities are important because they get participants interacting with one another and aid them in internalizing versus intellectualizing what you are trying to assist them in becoming aware of. You can pick and choose from activities you've tried before, create new ones, use activities other facilitators have developed, or adapt an existing activity to meet your audience needs. Our *Activities for Trainers* CD is available on our website at www.culturesconnecting.com/products, which provides you with instructions for facilitating a number of effective activities. You can also browse the website and find a wealth of diversity resources.

- *Lecture*. How much content knowledge should you prepare to deliver? Lecture is useful when done right, in that it can provide much needed content and context for the day and will help you to build credibility by demonstrating your content knowledge expertise. When you do take the opportunity to utilize this practice, make sure your lecture is engaging, interesting, and related to the objectives. We usually provide some mini lecture based on literature or research before or after an activity to provide context for what they will experience or have just finished experiencing.

- When using a PowerPoint to guide you, take the time to research how to develop an effective presentation. There is a great deal of information on the pitfalls of PowerPoint presentations. You don't want to lose their interest at a critical time of demonstrating your expertise because a boring PowerPoint causes them to miss important information. Keep in mind that not unlike children, most adults cannot process large chunks of information over a long period time. Lecture is an essential part of a workshop done well, but participants need a balance of content, context, and experiential activities. As often as possible, switch from a "sit and get" lecture format, to one where they are engaging and interacting with each other. Helping others move along the continuum of cultural competence does not occur solely through cognitive processing. Transformation occurs most often when participants have a personal, emotional connection to the information, and that comes about through doing and then processing their experiences.

- *Context paired with content*. How can you help paint a clearer picture of the content? Although activities and lecture are both valuable tools for learning, providing context is also important. With each activity and key information that you share with them, think through examples, stories, metaphors, or graphics that you can use to bring your points to life. This helps participants make meaning of new learning and keeps them engaged throughout the day.

4. **The Way Content Is Delivered**

   - *Timing*. This work is demanding and can take a lot from you and your participants. As the day goes on, everyone is likely to become more exhausted. As a result, give the bulk of any lecture or information you want to share at the beginning of the day, when participants can most easily sit and listen. Whenever possible, save activities that require participants to get up and move around the room or interact with each other for after lunch, when they are more likely to be tired or easily distracted.

   - *Vary the learning methods you utilize*. Incorporate a variety of types of activities, such as role-playing, video, think/pair/share, small and large group discussion, simulations, journaling, visual art, theater, and so on. This will make learning fun and interesting and will meet the different learning styles of the participants in the room.

   - *Keep participants engaged*. If participants have been listening for a while, give them at least a few minutes to process at their tables or in a pair/share format what they are hearing, rather than always having them engage in large group discussion where they ask questions or share thoughts and you respond. If you notice participants are becoming sleepy, have them stand up and lead them through a stretching exercise or call a break earlier than you had planned.

5. **Facilitating New Activities**

   - *Try new activities*. It's a proud moment when you design your own activity. A great way to develop something new is to read an article or book and create an activity based on that information. Once you have developed a draft, talk through your curriculum with someone who has some experience in this area and who can offer suggestions.

   - *Practice presenting*. When facilitating something for the first time, whether you designed it or are doing something you've seen done before, find an opportunity to practice presenting at a conference or with an organization where you are essentially working pro bono. Your audience doesn't have to know this is new for you. Offering it at no cost is a fair exchange for being able to try something new with them. Feedback from the participant evaluations can inform you on where it needs modification the next time you present that same curriculum. It takes us about 5 or 6 times before we become confident in facilitating new material.

   - *Adapt an existing activity*. There are a lot of great activities designed to move participants along the continuum of cultural competency. However, sometimes you will come across an activity that you would like to use, but it doesn't quite fit for your audience; that is, the curriculum was designed for an adult audience and you are working with youth, or the activity takes longer than you have time for. Whatever the case may be, think about ways in which you can adapt it. Just be sure to give credit where credit is due.

6. **Closing the Workshop**

- *Inspirational message.* Ending with a poem, spoken-word recording, or short video clip to provide a sense of formal closure to the day and inspiration for future work is a great way to end the day.

- *Evaluations.* Have participants complete evaluations (see Appendix G, "Sample Workshop Evaluation Form"). Evaluations can be a useful tool to help you grow in your skills as a facilitator and will provide you with necessary feedback when designing future workshops. A word of caution: wait a day or two before reviewing your evaluations. Depending on how invested you were in the workshops success, your confidence in presenting, and your level of vulnerability, one negative evaluation can sometimes leave you feeling like a failure. It can be easy to lose sight of the many positive comments while narrowly focusing on the 2 or 3 criticisms that are very likely to emerge even for the most seasoned facilitator, given the nature of this work.

- *Homework.* If you are going to continue working with the same group over time, consider homework you might have them do between workshops. It could be something as simple as having them observe their own behavior based on what they learned, engaging with someone who didn't attend the workshop so they can become skilled at articulating their understanding of racism, becoming cognizant of ways in which the environments they come into contact with perpetuate stereotypes, or having them read an article. Whatever you have them do, it should build on the work they've just done or lead them into the work you will be doing with them in the future. Remember to follow up with them the next time you come together on what they noticed, understood, saw, or did based on the homework.

- *Compliment the work they've done.* Tell them if they have done great work. Mention a few things that you observed them doing well that day as a group. For example, you can say, "I want to thank you for this opportunity to work with all of you. I felt like you really took this day seriously by challenging yourselves and one another without stomping on each other's heads. I got the sense that you wanted to leave having understood yourselves and others more deeply. Nice work!" Whatever you say, it needs to be an honest reflection of your experience of them so that when they hear you say it, they believe it. Your comments will not likely be true of every single person in the room, but they should speak to your experience of the majority.

### STOP AND REFLECT

What are one or two new things you will try when structuring your next workshop?

_____

_____

_____

_____

# Chapter Two

## Creating a Welcoming Environment

What your learners see, hear, and feel (and perhaps smell and taste!) when they arrive sets the tone for the rest of the session. You send a message to your learners which essentially says, "Welcome. I've been waiting for you."

—Dr. Joye Norris

*Prepare the room as if you are preparing for special guests to come into your home.*

Engaging in deep conversations about race can be challenging, so it's imperative that you do as much as you can to create a welcoming experience from the moment you first come into contact with your participants. This will relieve some of the anxiety your participants may be bringing and create a space where they start to feel they can take risks and open up to one another. Many people have told us that the music we have playing when they walked in made the room feel welcoming. But even something as seemingly simple as music can be tricky.

Far too often facilitators spend the majority of their energy on curriculum development and not enough time on the learning environment. Environment is only one contributor to your success, but it can make a big difference in the overall outcome. Following you will find suggestions for ways in which facilitators can create a space that is invitational and at the same time immediately launches participants into learning. Some of them may seem obvious or simple, but we feel it's worth mentioning. It can be relatively easy for someone to name what they don't like about an environment but harder when it comes to articulating what would make it welcoming.

### 1. Provide Driving Directions

Give clear driving directions to the location of the workshop, parking instructions, and, if needed, signs directing them to the room once they enter the building. When I was doing one of our workshops we hold open to the public, I unknowingly put the business office address in the reminder email as the location of the workshop. On the morning of the workshop, we received call after call from participants who were lost. Not only did participants arrive late and frustrated, but we ourselves were frazzled at the start of the workshop from having to navigate all of the details of setting up the room and at the same time handling phone calls. There's nothing like learning from your mistakes. That won't happen again!

9

### 2. **Have the Room Ready**

When planning for the day, it helps to develop a checklist of everything that you will need to bring. You won't want to forget to bring something that is essential to the success of the workshop, like your laptop or handouts. (See Appendix B, "Checklist of What to Bring.")

Arrive early enough so that you have plenty of time to set the room up before your guests start to arrive. You never know what technical problems you may encounter, and you will be thankful for the added time needed to address them if any do arise. Having the room ready in advance will create a welcoming feeling for participants and can ease some of the anxiety you may be experiencing as you mentally prepare to facilitate.

### 3. **Set Up a Resource Table**

Make available a resource table that includes recommended reading, videos, flyers of upcoming workshops and conferences, and other resource materials they can look at before the workshop and during breaks. Find a nice colorful tablecloth and a few decorations for aesthetics. Sometimes participants will ask for a recommended reading list. In an effort to be environmentally conscious, we limit the amount of resource lists we print but are always willing to email one to a participant if they email us with their request and specifics around what they are looking for. In this day and age of technology it is easy for most people to take a picture with their phone. In addition, your resource table will often serve as an unknowing catalyst for participants to engage you and one another.

### 4. **Use Quotes**

Including quotes on large poster paper all around the room, rotating them on a PowerPoint, or having them on small strips of paper at their tables is a great way to get them thinking about the issues you will be working with them on—the moment they walk in the door.

### 5. **Provide Coffee, Tea, Pastries, and/or Treats for Full-Day Workshops**

In many cultures, food is a way to make guests feel welcome in your home. Providing food in your workshops can create this same feeling, and it keeps participants nourished throughout the day. We usually don't provide lunch but will offer coffee, tea, continental breakfast, and afternoon snacks. Initially, we only ordered caffeinated coffee to save money and because it was what we drank. During one particular workshop, a participant thoughtfully expressed her disappointment that there was no decaf available. We didn't realize the importance of this, as is so often the case when you don't look outside our your own needs or desires. Having realized the significance, one of us went to the nearby coffee shop while the other was presenting and brought her back a cup of decaf. She was surprised by the gesture. As a result of this experience, we always include decaf no matter how small the group. Again, lessons learned. Your participants will feel cared for by the effort you have made to consider their needs.

### 6. **Put Posters on the Wall**

Take the time to put up relevant discussion prompts, quotes, or information you may want to refer to at some point during the workshop. These can become nice visuals for participants to look at throughout the day, it creates a welcoming environment, and helps guide you on things you want to say but can't always remember. We have seen some facilitators who put the agenda on the poster paper rather than providing each participant with an agenda. They would then go back and review throughout the day what has been covered up to that point and then cross out anything that they would not be able to get to before time ran out.

### 7. Use PowerPoint

Have something on the screen—a cartoon, welcoming statement, rotating quotes, or inspirational messages that they can appreciate and/or learn from while they wait for the workshop to get started.

### 8. Meet and Greet Participants

When the room is set up in advance, it frees up your time to meet participants as they arrive. We walk around introducing ourselves, shaking hands with those we are meeting for the first time and offering up hugs to familiar faces when culturally appropriate. Reaching out to others in these ways may not feel comfortable for you. However, if you practice it enough times, eventually it will become like second nature. You will learn to pick up on subtle cultural cues that will help you to discern when and with whom these types of interactions are appropriate. There will be those moments when you find yourself standing and waiting for two participants to finish talking or when you say hello to someone for the second time not realizing that you had already greeted that same person at the door. In any case, you will find creative ways of making light of these and other awkward moments you are sure to encounter in this intimate exchange of pleasantries.

It won't always be possible to greet everyone before it's time to get started. But those you are able to meet and greet will most often respond positively to your energetic "I'm so glad you came today" tone of voice that leaves them feeling that you are genuinely happy to see them. This may be the only time that someone made them feel special that day—or that week. Thus begins the relationship-building process with your audience. This practice of engaging to make participants feel welcomed is something we now do consistently. It's effective, and it gives us an opportunity to know who's in the room.

### 9. Seat Participants whereby Engaging Is Optimal

Having round or square tables fitting 4 to 6 participants per table or sitting semicircle without tables so participants can easily see and engage one another is most conducive to learning. This helps to create a sense of community and circumvents the idea that you are the only one in the room with expertise, which often gets conveyed in lecture-type set-ups.

### 10. Have Music Playing

Select music that most everyone will appreciate or can relate to. Have it playing softly in the background before the workshop has begun. Sometimes we will choose music to make a point relevant to the workshop. For example, if you are doing a workshop on working with Latin@s,[1] consider playing music by Latin@ artists and then tie it into what you understand about the role of music in the Latin@ community. Another way to use music as an instrument for learning is to play music that not everyone will appreciate. As an example, you might play rap and then have participants reflect on whether or not they noticed it and how it made them feel. You can then discuss the importance of creating a welcoming environment in the workplace or what inclusivity looks like for different people.

### 11. Provide Name Tags

The participants may know one another if you are facilitating for an organization. However, this is not always the case. If there is a chance that they don't all know each other or if you won't be able to memorize all their names, have table tents or name tags so that everyone can

---

1. The @ symbol is used to denote Latino/Latina.

address each other by name and so you can avoid the embarrassment of not remembering. Calling someone by name personalizes the conversation, whereas saying "the guy in the blue shirt" or referring to participants as "sweetie," "sweetheart," or "honey," though meant to be endearing, can be insulting to some individuals.

### 12. Put Baskets in the Center of Tables

You can often find small baskets at your local dollar or craft store. Fill them with highlighters, pens, Post-it notes, 3 x 5 cards, treats, and other things participants may need during the workshop, and place one in the center of each table. This helps to create an atmosphere of learning and at the same time provides them with what they will need for the day. We attended one workshop where the organizers had placed different colorful squares of fabric underneath the baskets at the center of each table. This produced a wonderful ambiance in the room.

### 13. Place Norm Cards at the Center of Each Table

Have norm cards printed up in the shape of a table tent that you can place at the center of each table. They serve as a reminder for what participants can expect from themselves and others during the conversation, particularly when situations become challenging. (See Appendix C, "Norms.")

### 14. Have Something for Them to Leave With

Providing journals for participants to reflect in throughout the workshop, or giving away bookmarks or pens with your business information are great small gifts for them to have when they leave. At the end of the day, we will sometimes have participants choose a rock they will keep and have them reflect on a question; for example, "Choose a rock to take with you that signifies your solid commitment to change." We realize that purchasing gifts is not always an option, but when it is, it doesn't have to be costly. We make the journals and bookmarks with social justice quotes, and we find rocks on the beach, at garage sales, and at secondhand stores. Be creative. It adds a nice touch. Participants like leaving with something in hand.

### STOP AND REFLECT

1. Describe an environment that you were in that didn't feel welcoming. What made it unwelcoming?
2. What about it made you feel welcomed?
3. What else could be done to make an environment welcoming to you?

_____

_____

_____

_____

_____

_____

_____

_____

# Chapter Three

## Common Facilitator Fears and Needs

I must not fear. Fear is the mind-killer. Fear is the little-death that brings total obliteration. I will face my fear. I will permit it to pass over me and through me. And when it has gone past I will turn the inner eye to see its path. Where the fear has gone there will be nothing. Only I will remain.

—Frank Herbert, *Dune*

*Own your fears.*

**I**t's normal to experience a little anxiety when doing something that is important to you and when you want to be successful at it. A moderate amount of anxiety is usually helpful, but too much can be paralyzing. Your fears and anxiety about facilitating will only lessen with practice and time. We tend to experience more anxiety when facilitating new workshops than with ones we have done repeatedly. Bringing your fears to a level of consciousness, naming them, and then reflecting on them is one way to help you counter them.

Here is a list of fears and needs to help you uncover what's at the core of your anxiety:

1. **Fears:** Mark all the fears that you have felt about facilitating; add any others.
   ___ I will lose credibility and be seen as less competent.
   ___ The conversation will get out of control.
   ___ People will get too emotional, and I won't have the skills to manage the situation.
   ___ I won't know enough about the issue to effectively facilitate the conversation.
   ___ If I challenge the issue, participants will disengage.
   ___ If I am too confrontational, then people will be mad at me, reject me, ostracize me, etc.
   ___ I will be seen as incompetent and "not good enough."
   ___ I will reveal my own prejudice, bias, etc.
   ___ I'll let people down and disappoint them.
   ___ People won't like me or approve of me.
   ___ Things won't change. I'll be unable to make a difference.
   ___ I will make a mistake and be wrong.
   ___ If I don't handle this well, people will be hurt.
   ___ If I open up and share my experiences, people won't care.

___ I will create division among participants rather than bring them closer together.
___ I will look incompetent.

2. **Needs:** Mark all the needs you have when facilitating; add any others.
___ Need to be in control
___ Need for power and authority
___ Need to be accepted and included
___ Need to be seen as competent
___ Need to change and "fix" others
___ Need to be appreciated
___ Need to be right
___ Need to do things perfectly
___ Need for prestige and status
___ Need for recognition
___ Need for certainty and predictability
___ Need to be liked
___ Need for peace and harmony
___ Need for approval

### STOP AND REFLECT

1. What increases your fear (e.g., fatigue, illness, crises, stress at home, etc.)?
2. Where do your fears stem from (e.g., past events, experiences, traumas, upbringing)?
3. What behaviors do you sometimes exhibit when your needs aren't met (e.g., overcompensate, become angry, passive-aggressive behavior, become silent)?

Adapted from curriculum developed by Kathy Obear, Alliance for Change.

_____

_____

_____

_____

_____

_____

_____

_____

# Chapter Four

## Increasing Your Confidence as a Facilitator

The man who has confidence in himself gains the confidence of others.

—Hasidic saying

*Cultural competence is a journey, not an event.*

**P**resenting on race issues can be difficult for even the most skilled facilitators. We rarely, if ever, do our best the first, second, or even third time we try something. It's with practice that our skills develop. And no matter how much practice we have in facilitating an activity, the experience is never identical. While there are some things that we can expect to occur, we can never fully prepare for who is in the room and what may happen as a result. But, even with the anxiety-provoking surprises that will undoubtedly arise, there is always one thing we can anticipate—we will learn from the experience and become better facilitators as a result. Sometimes you just have to jump in and hope for the best, knowing that you have done everything possible to prepare for a successful outcome. Don't let what you don't know or the skills you haven't yet developed be the reason why you won't step into the role of facilitator. Participants are more likely to trust that you will be able to handle challenging situations when you believe in your abilities and bring your confidence into the space. Know that you have something valuable to offer, remember that there is a first time for everything, and, in the meantime, fake it till you make it.

1. **Recognize the Benefits of Facilitating**
   - *Facilitating is rewarding and growth promoting.* Preparing curriculum requires that you think through content. It helps to solidify your understanding of the subject. When you take it a step further and teach others, new learning for you always occurs. Participants will inevitably share their experiences and understanding of the issue,

which in return deepens your understanding. You can then take what you learned from participants to the next workshop you facilitate. Each time this happens you develop your expertise.

- *You'll learn more about yourself, others, and this work.* Reading about race and social justice issues is a helpful practice to deepen your knowledge. However, learning about self and others happens best in relationship. To actually experience your stereotypes playing out in a situation brings about a type of understanding of self that cannot be found in books. You can then use your experiences to provide context and invite others to explore their stereotypes and the impact. For example, I was once meeting with potential clients, two women of color and a white man. I was informed that one reason I didn't get the contract was that I paid more attention to the white man than I did the women of color. Initially I felt defensive. But given how important critical reflection is in this work, I began to pay closer attention to my cross-cultural interactions and could see this same dynamic repeat itself. It didn't matter that I identify as a woman of color. I can now appreciate the gift this person gave me. I learned a lot about the impact that my stereotypes have on others. As a result, I am able to share this experience in my workshops and name it the moment it occurs and invite others to do the same.

- *It will enhance your own abilities to effectively engage across cultures.* With practice comes experience. With experience comes skill. Essentially, the more you interact with people who have experiences that differ from your own, the more you learn. Facilitating workshops has provided us with opportunities to engage with all types of people from different cultural backgrounds, and as a result we have become more aware and skilled in our ability to effectively engage. You will too.

## 2. Remember That There's a Beginning for Everyone

- *There's a first time for everything.* It's important that when starting out you believe that you have some knowledge or information that your participants can benefit from. Your goal is to teach them what you have come to understand about a certain issue or topic and find ways for them to come to their own understanding. If you provide participants with opportunities to engage in open dialogue with you and the other participants, it will open the door for new learning to occur.

    It's normal when first starting out to question your ability to facilitate courageous conversations. You may question whether you have enough knowledge to share with others or if you have the skills to effectively deliver. While we believe that some people are indeed gifted in their ability to facilitate (e.g., their humor, style, ability to connect, etc.), with practice you can develop content-based knowledge and facilitation skills that will benefit your audience.

## 3. Take Risks and Welcome Your Mistakes

- *Take risks and experience discomfort.* Taking risks is a necessary part of becoming a skilled facilitator. It involves trying things you've never done before; sometimes planned, oftentimes in the moment. Of course, your anxiety will be high, and it's not uncommon to doubt your abilities. However, taking risks pushes you in ways that lead to growth. Think about the first time you learned to ride a bike. You probably needed training wheels. Eventually the extra wheels were removed. You may have crashed into a bush or two, but before long you were riding with ease. At a certain point you started shouting to your friends, "Look, no hands!"

- *Growth happens when we make mistakes.* Some participants will give us pushback when we use the word "mistake" to describe a situation where we were unconsciously or consciously incompetent. Rather than get caught up in this particular language, we want to convey the idea of embracing the fact that no one is perfect in this work. The best you can do is own whatever mistakes you make along the way and the impact they have on others. Being a facilitator puts you out in front of others, making it difficult to hide. Eventually you will do or say something that will offend someone. In these situations, practice asking questions to gain understanding, own it, learn from it, and try not to make the same mistake again—though, of course, there are no guarantees that you won't. When you do, recognize that it takes time to unlearn patterns of behavior and give yourself grace. We recently facilitated a two-day workshop open to the public. Our day-one evaluations expressed a concern about our use of "you guys." Neither of us was certain which one of us had been using it. I use it so automatically and unconsciously that I had never considered this language as gender-inappropriate. On the second day, it came up in discourse. Even after some participants shared their offense at the language, I continued to use it unknowingly. Had a participant not come up to me after the workshop to share how angry she was with me for "dismissing" their concerns, as evidenced for her by my continued use of the word, I would have never known that I was still saying it.

  It's helpful if you process afterwards with a friend or colleague what went wrong and brainstorm ways to improve the next time you have the opportunity to facilitate. We operate under the premise that situations that are challenging for you will come up again and again until you work through it. In other words, you will get another chance to do it again, like it or not. So be prepared!

## 4. Avoid Approaching This Work as an Expert

- *None of us are really "experts" in this work.* Facilitating conversations on race is too complex for anyone to completely master. However, over time, you can develop expertise. Seeing yourself as someone who has some expertise rather than being an expert will alleviate some of the burden you might place on yourself to "have to" know all things about all cultures and to handle all situations with ease. When a question or challenging situation arises that you are not sure how to address, you will be more likely to take an invitational approach that invites others into discourse rather than feeling the pressure to be the one with all the answers.

- *Welcome the expertise that your participants bring to the subject.* We refer to ourselves as facilitators, not trainers, for a reason. You are not "training" people on race relations like you might when teaching how to use a new software program. Your role is to facilitate dialogue and engage participants in a way that invites in their experiences and knowledge of the topic. This takes some of the responsibility off you to have all the answers or the "right" way of thinking and allows teaching and learning to occur from and for different participants in the room.

- *Share your experiences.* Your experiences shape your worldview and the lens through which you have come to understand race relations. Sharing them with participants can bring relevance and meaning to others, personalizes it by making you human and a part of the learning process, and helps participants see that everyone has something to bring to the conversation—a story.

## 5. Keep Your Fears and Anxiety to Yourself

- *Participants need to trust you will handle whatever occurs in the room.* Participants can't see or hear what's going on inside of you, so don't tell them how afraid and anxious you are feeling. It's not helpful for them to know this. Participants need to trust that you are able to facilitate the conversation before they will be willing to take risks and be vulnerable. They are less likely to open up and engage one another if they sense that you don't have the fortitude to manage challenging situations.

  Talking about a past experience when you were afraid can be helpful as a way to validate a similar feeling they have. But telling them you are afraid at that moment diminishes their feeling of safety and trust. There are times when you can share what you are feeling but only after you have built credibility and have demonstrated your ability to handle challenging situations.

## 6. Accept Resistance to Change

- *Expect Resistance.* More often than not you will have, at the very least, one participant resistant to growing in their understanding of racism, power, and oppression. Not everyone will have a positive attitude or be open to new learning. Encountering resistance is a part of the work. Accept that there will be resistance, and practice developing skills to address it.

  Resistance isn't always communicated verbally. Sometimes it shows itself in tone of voice, the folding of arms or rolling of eyes, where participants choose to sit and with whom they sit, inattentiveness, and other forms of disengagement. Resistance can also show up at the end of the day, when participants can remain anonymous about their true feelings in their evaluations.

  Remember, playing a part in reshaping the attitudes, beliefs, and behaviors of your fellow human beings happens over time. There will be always be those participants who support what you are doing and are open to learning, and there will always be those who refuse to be moved. Don't take this as a direct result of something you did or didn't do. Recognize that people believe what they believe for a reason and you won't come along and magically change their point of view. With some participants, your best hope is to plant seeds, making it easier for the next person who tries to engage them.

- *Think about someone you respect that faced challenges but stayed with it.* Remembering the challenges of great leaders like Martin Luther King Jr., Mahatma Gandhi, or people you may know personally who overcame obstacles and difficult situations can be helpful in building your confidence. Speaking affirmations like "They did it, and their challenges were so much greater than mine, I can do this too" can aid in assuaging your anxiety.

## STOP AND REFLECT

1. What's one thing you can do or say to yourself to boost your confidence when you feel apprehensive?
2. Who is someone you admire that has led social change work? What did you admire about him or her?

_____

_____

_____

_____

_____

_____

_____

_____

_____

_____

_____

_____

# Chapter Five

## Introductions

If we are to achieve a richer culture, rich in contrasting values, we must recognize the whole gamut of human potentialities, and so weave a less arbitrary social fabric, one in which each diverse human gift will find a fitting place.

—Margaret Mead

*Spend a long time preparing your introduction and a short time delivering it.*

**Y**our introduction sets the tone for the workshop and helps to establish your credibility with the group. This should be carefully planned so participants trust your leadership and the process, feel connected to you, and are committed to the goals of the day. Sometimes facilitators will take up too much time in delivery trying to set the stage, but it comes across as disjoined and incoherent. Valuable time is being wasted that should be used for participants later in the day to converse with one another, engage the materials, and process new information. This is most common among beginner facilitators who are feeling the anxiety and fear that navigating race conversations often elicits. In many cases, it is an unconscious, unintentional way to avoid moving forward. You may worry that you won't have enough knowledge and information to fill up the allotted time you are given, but, in actuality, once you get going you will find that both you and your participants have more to share than time allows. Spend a significant amount of time preparing your introduction and a short time delivering it so that you present in a manner that is clear, concise, and to the point. Then trust yourself and the agenda you have carefully prepared and stick with it rather than filling up airtime trying to relieve your anxiety.

### 1. Introducing Yourself

- *Keep it brief.* Done well, you should be able to introduce yourself in 5 to 10 minutes. How much time you spend will in some ways depend on how much time you have to facilitate the workshop. Whether you have a half day, full day, or only a few hours, time is precious, so carefully plan what you want to share. Like everything else, you will get better with time. It's normal to feel nervous at the start of a workshop. Having a well-practiced, concise introduction can ground you in the work and helps you to relax and transition into the day.

- *Tell a story that connects the audience to you, to each other, and to the work.* There are many creative ways you can connect the audience to you. One way is to show pictures of yourself, family members, and others who have helped shape your racial/ethnic identity in a PowerPoint. This can assist you in staying on track and is a great visual for participants as you allow your story to unfold. Another strategy is sharing your own "Where I'm From" poem. This is based on a poem by George Ella Lyon and the lesson plan by Linda Christensen in her book *Reading, Writing and Rising Up*. Not only is this an effective way to introduce yourself, it also assists you in critically reflecting on your own process, who you are, and why you are committed to social justice work. However you choose to share your story, it should leave your audience feeling like they know you better and increase their trust in you. Becoming culturally competent is a journey, so model for them that you are on this journey right along with them rather than coming across as the "expert" or someone who has "arrived" in their cultural competence. This will go a long way in getting participants to open up with you and one another.

- *Being introduced by someone else.* If you are doing a workshop for an outside agency and the person who brought you in offers to read your biography, ask them instead to talk about why their organization is committed to doing this work. Reading biographies tends to be impersonal and can distance your audience from you. Don't be shy about asking them to add something short about their interactions with you and why they invited you to facilitate. This approach will be more relevant to participants and is a useful way to begin the conversation. After they have introduced you, share the more personal introduction of yourself that you planned.

## 2. Setting the Stage

- *Review the norms for courageous conversations.* These norms (See Appendix C, "Norms.") are based on the work of Glenn Singleton, but we have added to them and developed our own definitions based on our experiences and understanding. Norms are essential in helping participants know what to expect of themselves and each other throughout the workshop. Whenever you work with a new group, discuss each norm at the beginning of the workshop. When working with a group over time, you can shorten this process by reviewing a few norms, particularly those that may be most relevant to the day.

- *Explain how you facilitate.* Sometimes it can be helpful to explain to participants your facilitation style so they know what to expect. This strategy is beneficial if your facilitation style involves a more direct approach or is uncharacteristic as a way to challenge participants to grow and take risks. By knowing what to expect, they will be less likely to feel singled out in the moment. Below are some examples of things that can be advantageous to share if they are a part of your approach to facilitation.

  *I will allow time for silence to give you time to think about how to respond.*
  *I will do my best to challenge you to go deeper.*
  *I will take risks to facilitate us through courageous conversations that may generate discomfort in all of us.*
  *If things get tense between participants, I may coach you through challenging situations to help you better engage one another.*
  *I will call on people that haven't had a chance to speak.*
  *I will call on you even if you haven't volunteered to speak.*

## 3. **Review the Objectives for the Day**

- *Explain your objectives for the workshop up front.* Your objectives inform participants what you hope to accomplish for the day. This lets them know what to expect and what not to expect. Having an objective stating that "participants will," for example, "increase their understanding of how racial stereotypes impact learning" helps convey the message that the focus of conversation will be on race versus some other form of oppression.

  State your objectives up front so if participants get off track you can remind them of the objectives. For example, if someone brings up class issues, you might say something to this effect: "Class is an important topic that also needs to be addressed, along with many other types of oppression. These issues do intersect because people have multiple identities. However, for the purpose of our objectives today and because of the limited time we have, I'm going to keep us focused on race with the understanding that they overlap and are multifaceted."

- *Exploring what participants hope to learn in your workshop.* Once you begin the workshop, it can be difficult to make significant changes to the agenda. We don't recommend using the time to explore what participants hope to gain if you are not in a position to adapt the day around what they are wanting. This can cause disappointment and impact your credibility.

  If you do ask what they hope will be covered, be prepared to respond when they indicate something you don't plan on tackling. If possible, find out what they are hoping for in the planning phase. Usually, this isn't feasible unless you are working with the same group over time, in which case you can always address their needs in follow-up sessions. A question in the evaluation that asks what else they would like to learn can also inform the development of future lesson plans.

  One benefit in asking this question is that as you are presenting you can emphasize areas that are connected to what they hoped to learn. It can help you to remember to address specific issues by putting it up on poster paper and labeling it "Parking Lot." However, a common problem with using a parking lot approach is that you may not have time to go back and address what they wanted you to address. One way to avoid this parking lot problem is to tie its use into the "Expect and Accept Nonclosure" norm. You can do this by informing participants that you may or may not get to what's on the parking lot, but that at the very least it will serve as a reminder for all of the issues and concerns we need to be addressing as a society.

- *Use a framework for cultural competence.* Providing participants with a framework for cultural competence will assist you in explaining what "this work" requires of us. Regardless of whether participants have attended race-related workshops with other facilitators, it will be important for you to all have a common framework, language, and understanding for the work that you will be doing together. We have found the work of Derald and David Sue paired with Judith Katz to be most beneficial in defining and painting a clear picture of cultural competence. If you have an entire day, we recommend taking anywhere from 60 to 90 minutes covering this topic. If you don't have that much time to dedicate, use the cultural competence graph we created (see page 5) to briefly go over the four areas. Once you have reviewed the four components of cultural competence, explain which area you will be focusing on in your time together. Sometimes your workshop content will cover more than one area.

## 4. **Participants Introducing Themselves to Each Other**

- *Steer clear of having individuals introduce themselves to the entire group.* Even if you only have 15 participants in your workshop, going around one at a time having each person do a typical 2-minute introduction of their name, their department, and how long they have been in the organization can take up valuable time. This would take up 30 minutes of workshop, not to mention those who take more than the allotted time given, easily taking you to a 45- to 60-minute introductory session. Instead, we recommend that you give participants a set amount of time to introduce themselves to their table groups using a prompt you provide. Here are some possible prompts:

*Take 2 minutes each to go around your tables and briefly share ...*
- ... your name, where you work, and what you hope to get out of the day.
- ... your name, how long you have worked for this company, and how you feel about being here today.
- ... your name, where you work, and your past experiences in having conversations about race.

Sometimes it's helpful to emphasize the importance of not taking more than the allotted time so that they understand that not everyone will get a chance to share if one person dominates. This is also a time to recognize if the tables are unevenly distributed. Take a risk and ask participants to volunteer to move to another table if there is a table with only two participants and another table with six. Explain that you are asking them to move so that everyone gets enough time to share throughout the day. This might create some discomfort or frustration, particularly if they are sitting with friends. Encourage them anyway. If participants don't respond to your request, approach the table and kindly request that someone join the table with only two participants. It may not make you the most popular person with a few individuals, but in addition to serving its purpose, it will also establish your leadership in the room.

## TRY TO AVOID

- Making self-deprecating remarks that leave them with the impression you don't know what you're doing.
- Minimizing what you bring to the experience. This is difficult, on-going work, and we are all learners, but you do have some insights to share, and participants need to believe you can facilitate them through the tough parts.
- Using fillers (unnecessary information) that take up airtime.
- Being worried that you won't have enough information for the day.
- Packing your agenda too tight and then moving too quickly through it to try to cover everything.
- Doing too much of the talking, which results in not enough time for participants to engage one another around the material. Processing is an important part of learning and helps participants internalize what they've been hearing.

Everything you say and do provides clues as to who you are, where you're going, and how you see the world.

—Advanced Leadership Communication

## STOP AND REFLECT

Write a short introduction that helps to establish your credibility and connects participants to you. Include a short anecdote from your life that ties in why this work is important to you personally.

_____

_____

_____

_____

_____

_____

_____

_____

_____

_____

_____

_____

# Chapter Six

## Building Relationships

Insight, I believe, refers to the depth of understanding that comes by setting experiences, yours and mine, familiar and exotic, new and old, side by side, learning by letting them speak to one another.

—Mary Catherine Bateson

*Connect, reconnect, connect, connect, and reconnect.*

**H**ow many times have you been to a workshop where you never learned the name of the person sitting next to you? How many times have you tried to have a deep conversation with a stranger? Individualism and competition are two of the norms of white culture that serve to reinforce white privilege by keeping us from working together for change. In order to undo institutional racism, we must make time to learn about each other, care about each other, and find ways to communicate across our divides.

Developing relationships with your participants and using activities where they can learn from and about one another is a necessary part of their growth. Time spent on this at the beginning and throughout the workshop will pay off later when participants trust they can share their thoughts and experiences with one another. The idea is to connect and reconnect as often as possible.

### 1. Understand Issues Underlying the Resistance

Your participants will bring various fears, negative past experiences, and a resistance to seeing themselves as they really are that will make relationship building imperative for a successful outcome. As participants experience cognitive dissonance or a challenge to their identity, they are likely to react defensively. The relationship you've built with participants will come into play as you try to guide them through difficult learning about themselves. It is helpful for facilitators to understand the deeper issues that may lie beneath the surface. Consider the following:

- *Naming the problem.* To dismantle institutional racism, individuals must change their behaviors and beliefs and develop new understandings of how systems of oppression work to preserve dominant cultural norms. Because our systems of injustice are so complex and have endured for so long, if individuals are not intentional about learning and growing in their understanding, regardless of their racial or cultural background, they will unconsciously maintain those systems. Inaction maintains the status quo. However, if we can change the way individuals see themselves and systems, we can change the policy and practice that sustains them and therefore cultivate a society grounded in equity and social justice.

- *Whites with friends of color.* One of the more difficult parts of change work is guiding participants through the process of becoming aware of their own bias, stereotypes, privilege, and behaviors that are heavily imbedded in colorblind ideology. Many of the white participants in your workshop will have spent a lifetime developing what they believe to be a nonracist identity founded in their relationship with people of color. Those relationships become proof of their truth that they are somehow immune to racial socialization. An example of this is the white person who says, "My best friend is black" or "My children are biracial" in response to anyone who begins to suggest that they are not as enlightened as they think they are. These types of statements allow white people to distance themselves from historical oppressions, white supremacists, and racist family members and friends. Unfortunately, it also prevents them from doing the necessary personal work of exploring their own unconscious bias.

- *Participants of color who have assimilated.* It's not uncommon to have at least one participant of color who has developed an identity immersed in white cultural norms and who has bought into the myth of meritocracy. This person may believe assimilation will create racial equity. They don't believe talking about racism is necessary and often will use their own successful experiences as proof that people of color are making excuses for their problems.

- *White participants who have had negative past experiences.* Whites have had a multitude of negative experiences around race that have left them wounded as a result of trying to engage people of color. They often feel that no matter what they do or say, they will always be personally blamed for racism. Past conversations may have led them to believe their efforts will never be enough to build their relationships with people of color and be seen as allies. This can result in feelings of powerlessness, shame, and guilt, paralyzing them when faced with the opportunity for meaningful conversation that can lead to personal growth. They may fear that any misstep will further the racial divide or expose them in some way as racist.

- *People of color who are tired of trying.* There are people of color who have been doing this work for a long time and who are tired of trying to help white people understand that racism still exists. They have shared story after story, trying to convince white people to see what they refuse to see only to be met with statements like "How do you know that's what she meant?" or "Don't you think you're making too much of this?" and "I had that same experience, so it's not about your race." Not only have they come to believe that another workshop won't make a difference, they also don't want to defend their experiences as truth one more time. The cost feels too high. Every time people of color share an experience of racism, they relive that story. When people invalidate their experiences, it brings up the anger and pain all over again.

In effect, both groups can enter into these conversations with fear and trepidation looming in the background. Knowing this, it's important from the beginning that you begin to build social capital with every participant so that they trust you will be able to navigate these perilous waters. They need to be reassured their experience together will be different, and building relationships is a crucial step in helping to mitigate their underlying fears.

## 2. **What Is Social and Community Capital?**

Imagine you come to the workshop holding an empty bucket. The bucket symbolizes your relationship with participants, and the fact that it starts out empty symbolizes their negative past experiences with race relations. Now, picture having a positive interaction with a person in the room because of something you said or did. A chip is deposited into your bucket as a result. The goal is to have accumulated enough chips in your bucket so when something doesn't go as planned, you make a mistake, or you are met with inevitable resistance, you are able to withdraw a chip from the bucket so participants remain willing to stay engaged.

Filling the bucket can start with your first contact, through phone calls, registration, emails, and so on, and will continue throughout the workshop as you demonstrate your ability to lead and facilitate courageous conversations. You can also build social capital with participants you are not directly interacting with but who witness your interactions with someone else in the room. On the other hand, consider you have no social capital with participants in the room. In other words, your bucket is empty. When you make a blunder or don't handle a situation effectively, you will have nothing to draw out to cause them to trust you.

Community capital is similar to social capital, except it applies to participants' interactions with one another. The more activities you engage them in that allow them to get to know one another and build on their relationships, the more they will be willing to give one another grace when offensive comments are made, to steer clear of attacking behaviors, and to engage in ways that meet each other where they're at. It is much more effective when individuals join together to advocate for change than it is for one or two people to try to organize social justice work.

Change doesn't require that everyone get on board, but we certainly benefit from a larger crew. Taking time to invest in our relationships with one another builds the foundation needed to work together.

In all the situations described above, remember that people are likely to be hurting and afraid. Listen well. Ask questions with genuine curiosity to find out more about where they are coming from and what their experiences have been that led to their resistance. In other words, build relationships through understanding. This will increase your chances of their opening up to the experience of the day.

## STRATEGIES FOR BUILDING RELATIONSHIPS

Some of the strategies below may stretch you to move outside your comfort zone. Although you don't want to appear inauthentic in your relationship building, keep in mind facilitating a workshop is different from any other social situation. If relationship building doesn't come naturally for you, try one new strategy and practice it to a point of comfort before incorporating the next.

### 1. **Welcome Participants as They Enter the Room**

- *Stand near the door and greet each participant with a handshake or a hug.* Welcoming participants as they enter the room is a nice way to show you are glad to have them there. It can also help to alleviate any thoughts they may have about you being a distant facilitator who is unconcerned about their well-being.

- *Walk around the room and introduce yourself to participants.* It's unlikely you will be able to greet every participant at the door as they enter the room. Some participants will have already arrived by the time you are finished setting up. Others will get past you while you are speaking to someone else. One way to ensure you have had some contact with every person in the room is to go around to the different tables and introduce yourself. Welcome them to the workshop by asking their name and either what organization they come from or what their role is within an organization. In addition to giving you the opportunity to connect and build relationships, it will also help you get an idea of who is in the room. Take note of their nonverbal communication. This will provide insight into their attitudes about being there. If you are facilitating for an organization you work for, going around and greeting everyone in the room is an effective strategy for connecting with staff you don't know and reconnecting with those you do.

## 2. Show Participants They Matter to You

- *Gently touch a participant on the shoulder.* The simple act of touching someone on the shoulder can have a powerful positive effect. There are five ways we use shoulder touch during a workshop: (1) touching a shoulder while introducing yourself to someone sitting at a table; (2) touching a shoulder while speaking directly to a person you are sharing a laugh with or whom you are engaging in a non–anxiety-provoking conversation; (3) touching a shoulder when coaching or engaging an individual in courageous conversation; (4) touching a shoulder of someone while addressing the larger group, particularly when someone is standing or sitting next to you and you are unable to look at them and the rest of the participants at the same time; and (5) touching a shoulder to interrupt a small group conversation. There may be a participant who is not comfortable with touch. Pay close attention to their nonverbal cues. If you get the sense touch is not okay for someone, don't let your hand linger on their shoulder. If it's obvious they are not okay with your touch, simply apologize for taking the liberty, remove your hand, and continue the dialogue. However, we have found in most cases, a gentle touch on the shoulder is a great strategy for creating a personal connection between you and your participants.

- *Call participants by name.* Calling participants by name or coming up with a nickname based on something brilliant they said in the workshop is another helpful relationship building tool. Knowing someone's name helps to create a feeling of connectedness. It shows you see them and that they matter to you. Having each participant wear a name tag is helpful if you are working with a large group or if you have trouble remembering names. When using nicknames, avoid calling participants "dear" or "honey." There are many people who don't like to be referred to in this way. No matter how good your intentions, it can feel condescending. However, a nickname can help build a relationship when it is meaningful. You might come up with something playful as a result of what a person said or did in the workshop. It should always convey a positive message about what that individual brought to the conversation. We attended a workshop together once where by the end of the day the facilitator had given almost every single participant a name, such as "Dr. Jones," "Insightful One," or "Teacher."

- *Give someone a sincere compliment for the work they're doing.* Participants are taking risks to speak openly about their thoughts, feelings, and attitudes related to race and social justice issues. Complimenting reinforces their engagement in a healthy way and encourages them to continue to take risks.

- *Bring up key points participants made throughout the workshop.* Showing that other people in the workshop contribute to the learning process encourages participants to share their best thinking. It implies you are not the only one with expertise in the room and speaks to the value of different voices. For example, when talking about a subject, make connections between what you are sharing and what someone else said earlier. For example, "This speaks to the point Julia made earlier when she said ____," or "Martin said it well when he mentioned      ."

- *Refer to ideas you've learned from participants in other workshops.* This speaks to the fact that we are building on the learning of others. It shows you learn from your participants and incorporate their ideas into your own thinking: "I showed this same slide to a group of high school students, and one of them who pointed out the fact that ____. I hadn't even thought about it in that way until she mentioned it."

3. **Give of Yourself and Be Vulnerable at Times**

- *Take risks.* When you share the norms with participants, there is a parallel process occurring. The same norms that apply to the participants, apply to you as the facilitator. There will be many opportunities for you to take risks, and you should not shy away from those moments for fear you will look incompetent. One way to take risks is to try something that you've never done before and to be transparent about it in the moment. Simply saying something to this effect: "I would like to try something I've never done before that I think will be helpful to you in this process," or "The interaction that just occurred between Reggie and me was difficult for me. I was nervous because I wasn't sure how it would turn out, but I'm glad I took the risk." This approach conveys you are equally willing to take risks in an effort to grow. It also helps participants see you as human rather than an expert who has all the answers.

- *Tell your own story.* It's important you don't create a divide between you and your participants that leaves them feeling embarrassed or ashamed for speaking their truth. You don't want to add to their fear that you will see their cultural incompetence in judgmental ways. Learning happens when people are able to openly explore the unconscious and bring it to a conscious level of awareness. Sharing challenges, mistakes, and even successes you have faced allows them to experience a part of your journey and the process you went through to get to where you are today. Telling a personal story as a way to introduce yourself is one way to do this. You can also incorporate your recent and past growth experiences throughout the workshop to make a point more meaningful. When asking participants to share their experiences, demonstrate or model by first sharing one of your own. However, be careful you don't take up too much time with storytelling. Leave them room to do their own exploring and processing.

- *Demonstrate a willingness to be vulnerable.* One of our greatest unspoken fears as human beings is that others will see us for who we really are, and won't like us. As a result, we put a lot of time and energy into creating an image we believe will put us in a favorable light, rather than being truthful about who we really are. The reality is that participants admire your vulnerability, particularly when it is balanced with a sense of competence rather than dominated by a persona of inadequacy. When you give of yourself in this way, it models what it means to be human and gives others permission to do the same.

In the course of a workshop there will be many opportunities for you to be vulnerable by revealing moments when you are learning, too. This can range from asking the definition of a word just spoken, to admitting out loud that you had never thought of something in a particular way before, to even allowing yourself to cry as you experience the pain of your own or another person's story. The key is balance. Too much confidence or too much vulnerability can damage the relationship and your credibility. Here are some examples of ways you can acknowledge when you are learning:

*I never thought of it that way before.*
*I'm going to use that information in my next session.*
*I didn't realize _____.*
*That's very interesting, do you know if _____?*

- *Giving of yourself invites others to do the same.* You have to give of yourself in the same way you are asking participants to give if you want them to trust you to lead them through the process of growing their awareness and understanding. Reflecting on a time when you thought the way they did conveys to them they won't be judged by you and reveals you understand because you have been there too. It also shows participants you are all in this together, just at different stages of the process.

- *Be present.* When a participant is speaking, it's easy to lose focus by mentally planning how you will respond. Work on being present so you can track what the person is or isn't saying with verbal and nonverbal communication. Your verbal and nonverbal body language should communicate you are engaged, especially when participants are being most vulnerable. It's all right if your response is not perfect or doesn't convey everything you wanted it to. Chances are high that later conversations will trigger key points you wanted to make, giving you the opportunity to address it at that time. The more you facilitate, the easier this will get, but even for the more seasoned facilitator this can be challenging. One strategy is to jot down brief notes of what participants are saying. This will help remind you of what you wanted to say. Note-taking is particularly helpful when you want to let several participants share without interruption.

## PROVIDE OPPORTUNITIES FOR PARTICIPANTS TO GET TO KNOW ONE ANOTHER

It is critical to provide opportunities for participants to develop relationships with one another. This requires opportunities where they can share something about their stories that ties into who they are or where they have come from. Then, as the day goes on and the conversations go deeper and more courageous conversations and critical reflection is involved, there is some context to why they see or feel the way they do about issues.

1. **Use Warm-Up Activities**
   - *Make time to socialize.* Encourage participants to show up early for food, coffee, and registration at least 30 minutes prior to the start of the workshop, so they have time to settle in and socialize with each other. This will also give you time to get to know who is in the room.

- *Post a prompt.* Not everyone is comfortable talking with people they don't know. As a way to encourage them to engage, post a question on the screen or on a poster paper as a way to encourage them to talk with one another before or throughout the workshop.

- *Icebreakers.* Have an icebreaker activity planned for the beginning of the workshop that will allow participants to begin to get to know one another, develop trusting relationships, and ease them into courageous conversations. This can be done through table talks or by having them move around the room and interact. Use activities that allow them to meet people early on in a short period of time. Once participants have interacted with each other, ask two or three people to share with the larger group either their experience of doing the activity or what they shared with others. You might ask, "What was the process of doing this activity like for you?"

## 2. Using Prompts

Prompts provide participants the opportunity to practice articulating their thinking about an issue you want them to explore more deeply and allow them time to process what they have just learned. We often have them respond to prompts in pairs or triads, allowing each person a set amount of time to talk, while the others listen without comment. This creates equality in time distribution. Prompts can also be used in small groups. Inform participants when time is running out so that everybody has the opportunity to share. There are a numerous occasions when prompts are particularly useful:

Before the workshop starts, post a question on the screen or large poster paper so as they enter the room, they are prompted to engage one another and begin thinking about the issues.

At the beginning of the workshop, right after you discuss the goals, objectives, norms, and your introduction, have them respond to a prompt to help them transition into courageous conversations.

Following an activity or lesson plan you just taught, or at the end of your time together, give them a prompt to allow them to think about what they know or feel about the topic, process new learning, or consider ways to apply what they've learned to their practice.

Examples of prompts include:

*How are you feeling about being here today and why?*
*Talking about race and racism is difficult for me because _____.*
*What's one thing you want people to know about you that they can't tell by looking at you?*
*When did you first realize your race mattered?*
*What does cultural competence mean to you?*
*What have been your experiences in having conversations about race?*
*What do you do well and what will you work on?*
*What's one thing you will do differently as a result of what you learned today?*
*How does this apply to the work you do?*

Whatever prompt you decide to use, be creative with the questions you ask and how you have them engage. The more opportunities you provide them to engage one another in conversation, the more likely they are to build trusting relationships and deepen their own thinking.

## TRY TO AVOID

- Doing all the talking, leaving little time for participants to get to know one another.
- Thinking about how to respond when it's a time to be listening.
- Referring to participants in ways that are belittling or offensive.

> Learning is finding out what we already know. Doing is demonstrating that you know it. Teaching is reminding others that they know just as well as you. You are all learners, doers and teachers.

> —Richard Bach

## STOP AND REFLECT

What are some strategies or activities that you have used or seen that work to build relationships among participants?

_____

_____

_____

_____

_____

_____

_____

_____

# Chapter Seven

## Establishing Credibility

Just because I am, doesn't mean I do understand. Just because I'm not, doesn't mean I don't.

—Jamie Washington

*Who am I to talk about racism? Who are you not to?*

Establishing credibility is a critical element to being an effective facilitator. Based on past experiences, participants will enter into your workshops at different places on a continuum of understanding and, as a result, will have varying attitudes about doing this work. In addition to creating a welcoming environment and building relationships, establishing credibility also helps to establish their trust in you to take them deep into personal reflection when it's necessary to do so. There are a variety of ways to demonstrate that you have done the necessary work that enables you to lead conversations on race. Showing you know how to facilitate and are unafraid to engage in courageous conversations will do far more to establish credibility than listing your degrees or years of experience. Establishing your credibility in the beginning and throughout the day will help to lessen participants' resistance during those times when you challenge them to explore the foundations of their thinking.

### 1. Take Control of the Workshop

Participants expect you to guide the conversation. They are likely to become frustrated if one or two people derail an activity or conversation and will look to you to interrupt the disruption so learning occurs for the majority rather than just a few. It can be challenging to figure out when to do this and with whom, particularly given that people of color tend to be highly relationship-oriented and often communicate through story. This can take up a lot of time and frustrate some of their white counterparts who tend to be more linear and agenda bound. It will be your role to stay attentive to those moments when processing is important. Not allowing enough time to process by moving too quickly through an activity can leave either party feeling as though they are not getting what they came for. These two different styles of communication, while not entirely culturally bound, can be difficult to navigate if you are not comfortable taking control of the room. There will be times when you will need to allow space for storytelling or processing and other times when it will be more advantageous to the entire group to redirect the conversation and get the participant quickly on point. There is no formula for knowing when to utilize which approach. However, as you get better at identifying when this is occurring and practice taking risks, you will grow in your ability to effectively facilitate. (See p. 44 for strategies for getting participants back on track).

### 2. **Take Risks to Challenge Participants to Go Deeper**

Asking questions about a participant's thoughts, feelings, and experiences that may have led to their comments, beliefs, or assumptions when they appear to be resistant to new information is the best approach to helping participants gain deeper insight. However, this strategy is not easy. Most of us are quick to judge and slow to wonder. Try to keep in mind this is about their development, not about you showing the audience how much you know, or convincing a particular person how wrong they are. Your goal in this moment will be to plant seeds in their mind that can potentially lead to a new way of thinking about and understanding race and other social justice issues. This may or may not occur in the moment but that doesn't mean change isn't happening.

In order to successfully help someone develop new insights, it's important that you find out why they believe, think, or feel the way they do even when you think you already know the reasons. The best practice is to ask questions that help participants arrive at their own understanding. What's most challenging about this approach is figuring out what questions to ask that will take them there. You will likely have to ask quite a few questions before one resonates with them in a way that shifts them from defensiveness to reflection. Here are some general questions you might try:

*What's going on for you right now?*
*How are you feeling about what you are hearing?*
*What were you taught to believe about ____?*
*Do you have any thoughts about how ____ might be influencing the way you are responding to this conversation?*
*Imagine if what Angie said was true. How would you feel?*
*What could you do to gain more insight so that you have broader perspective to work from?*
*Do you have any insight as to why it might be difficult to believe what others are telling you about their experiences?*

### 3. **Use Quotes and Tie in the Work of Those with Expertise in the Field**

When you refer to other people's work, it connects what you are teaching with the research and thinking of many people in the field who have been addressing these issues over a long period of time. It also provides those interested with resources that will further their knowledge and understanding beyond the workshop. One way white privilege is maintained is by valuing the individual over the collective experience and by taking credit for other people's ideas. Therefore, it's particularly important in social justice work that you recognize the ideas and thinking that are not your own. Citing others also conveys that you have done some of the necessary work to develop your own. Referencing can aid in those moments when a participant is resistant to new information. When you are speaking to research, not your own subjective thinking, they must challenge the research, not the messenger.

## 4. **Acknowledge Your Own Biases**

When doing cultural competency work over a long period of time, it is easy to forget how difficult it was when you first started looking inward and sharing with others what you've learned about your own shortcomings. Admitting your bias in front of an audience models for participants what it looks like to openly explore racial socialization and shows them how rewarding it can be, despite what they may be feeling in the moment. By talking about your own bias, attitudes, and beliefs, past and present, you give participants permission to do the same. One way to do this is to share some of the stereotypes you hold about your own group and groups you don't identify with, as well as instances when you recognized your bias.

For example, "Though I have older brothers who are white, I am inclined to make stereotypical assumptions about white men. I tend to see them as all coming from socially and economically advantaged backgrounds, even though from experience I know this isn't true." If you've gained credibility with your participants, naming your stereotypes will often heighten their respect for you. Another example might be naming your bias in the moment, "I just realized, when you mentioned technology, that I had an image of an Asian person in my head. I didn't realize it until you said she was Latina," or "When I asked you to ____, I just realized I had assumed that because you are ____, and thought you would be the best person to do it. It's another example of how I have to constantly be aware of my own bias."

## 5. **White Facilitators**

It's not unusual for white facilitators to feel pressure to do well. You are more likely to have the desire to prove to yourself and participants that you are qualified to facilitate conversations on race. Whites sometimes feel, "Who am I to talk about racism?" Try instead asking yourself, "Who are you not to?" It shouldn't be the burden of people of color to always initiate, lead, or facilitate race conversations. It is everyone's work to liberate our society from oppressive practices. We need people of color and whites to take on leadership roles to bring more and more people into the conversation in healthy ways.

Regardless of whether you are having this type of internal struggle, the moment participants realize their facilitator is white, they are likely to think, "You're white, what can you teach us about racism?" This can come from white participants, but most often it is the unspoken thoughts of participants of color.

A helpful strategy is to name this elephant up front. This can be done a number of ways. For example, you might ask early on in the workshop, "I'm wondering how many of you are surprised or are wondering what a white person is doing leading a workshop exploring racism?" You can have them raise their hands in response, though it's not necessary. The act of just naming it can dissipate some of the negative thoughts or feelings they may be having towards your whiteness. You can also have them briefly do a turn and talk and discuss their thoughts and feelings. In this case, inform them that they won't be asked to share their thoughts with the whole group; avoid listening in on conversations. The purpose is to let them know you know what they are likely to be thinking, that it's common, and that you are not afraid to talk about it. The simple act of naming something like this also can ease your own discomfort.

Another strategy is to wait until you begin to actually sense that a participant is challenging you because of your whiteness rather than what they are verbalizing in the room. In this instance you might say something like this: "I notice every time I give directions for an activity, you ask questions about why we're doing this and the impact it will have on people of color. I'm wondering if it's difficult for you to trust me to lead this process because I'm white?" This strategy is more difficult than naming it up front to everyone in general because it can create defensiveness, particularly if they are not willing to own their thoughts and feelings publicly. It is also likely that there are other participants in the room who feel the same way. Even if the participant you address doesn't acknowledge that it is your whiteness that is the issue for them, it does convey a message that you are not afraid to have courageous conversations. In the end, this can help you establish credibility and will likely diminish the possibility that they will challenge you at every turn.

If you try this second strategy, don't address the whole group as if your whiteness is getting in everyone's way. Participants will know whom you are really talking about. With this strategy, you will need to take risks and model courageous conversations by talking to a specific person, just like you are trying to teach them to do.

If you avoid naming this elephant altogether, participants are more likely to consciously or unconsciously act out on their unspoken thoughts by challenging you in ways they would not have challenged a facilitator of color. This shows itself when participants challenge everything you say and do, and it hinders the process.

*White facilitators can establish credibility with participants of color by ...*
- Sharing what you have learned about yourself in this work.
- Telling stories that acknowledge your own racial/ethnic identity development or privilege.
- Sharing experiences that changed your views ("Encounter" moments).
- Talking about being a white facilitator from the start and inviting participants to privately or publicly discuss how they are reacting to this fact (name the elephant in the room).
- Discussing the personal and professional work you have done in this area.
- Acknowledging people of color who have influenced your thinking personally and professionally.
- Speaking from your own experiences rather than the experiences of people of color.
- Being patient with building trust and not trying too hard to be accepted up front.
- Demonstrating your willingness to be a co-learner, rather than an expert with all of the answers.

### 6. Facilitators of Color

As a person of color it's normal to feel added pressure to do well. Due to stereotypes that convey that people of color (POC) are not as smart as whites, people of color can consciously or unconsciously feel the need to prove their intelligence. The threat of fulfilling this stereotype can increase fears and anxiety and affect performance. Understanding what might be happening internally and normalizing your experience can help to ease some of this stress. Claude Steele (2010, 88) states, "And when people with these identities are doing something, or are in a situation for which a negative stereotype about their group is relevant, they can feel stereotype threat; they can feel under pressure not to confirm the stereotype for fear that they will be judged or treated in terms of it."

When only a few participants of color are in the room, particularly from your own racial group, it increases the likelihood that you will feel a weightiness to do well so as not to embarrass them. They may be hoping or even silently praying that you are good at what you do. The pressure they experience in their organizations to counter negative stereotypes can get projected onto you. This unspoken, often unconscious, burden of having to represent your group can affect your performance, knowing that if you do poorly it could look bad for them. It's helpful, once you have built credibility and have a strong sense that things are going well, to name this elephant. You can either do this with the entire group as a learning opportunity for them to further understand the complexity of racial experiences or individually with a participant of color. Naming the experience can bring what is often unconsciously occurring in the room to a conscious level.

Facilitators of color are also more likely to be seen by white participants as "playing the race card." Even if this is not said out loud, white participants may feel like you are there to make them feel guilty about their privilege. It is helpful to talk about how institutional racism and white privilege hurts all people and the ways we all benefit from addressing these issues together. You may also share stories about your own experiences of privilege, as a man, able-bodied person, heterosexual, and so on. This shows your connection and understanding of how difficult it can be to take responsibility for our unearned advantages and will create a space where white participants can reflect with less defensiveness.

*Facilitators of color can establish credibility with white participants by ...*
- Demonstrating that you are not there to make them feel bad or guilty about being white.
- Sharing other areas where you hold unearned privileges, for example, heterosexual, class, race, gender, religion, and so on.
- Acknowledging areas where you still have room to grow.
- Talking about the need for co-liberation by making statements like this: "We all have work to do," "This is everyone's work," or "We can't know all things about all cultures, even our own."
- Sharing work you've done to come to your current place of understanding.
- Acknowledge times when you've offended in cross-cultural interactions.

## STOP AND REFLECT

Write about an experience you've had doing this work where you learned an important lesson. Think about how you might use this story to establish credibility.

_____

_____

_____

_____

_____

_____

_____

# SECTION II

# FOUNDATIONAL FACILITATING
# TIPS & STRATEGIES

We are our only hope for creating a future worth working for. We can't go it alone, we can't get there without each other, and we can't create it without relying on our fundamental and precious human goodness.

—Margaret Wheatly

# Chapter Eight

## Facilitation Style

My continuing passion is to part a curtain, that invisible shadow that falls between people, the veil of indifference to each other's presence, each other's wonder, each other's plight.

—Eudora Welty

### TOP 10 REASONS WHY IT'S DIFFICULT TO FACILITATE CONVERSATIONS ON RACE

1. Participants are at different levels in their ethnic/racial identity development and therefore at varying levels of understanding.
2. Dealing with differences elicits anxiety in individuals and tension across cultures, creating a battleground for conflict.
3. Participants come looking for quick fixes. They want the answers for what they can do differently rather than invest the time and energy in personal change that would lead to the answers they seek.
4. People refer to their own experiences to develop meaning of other people's experiences, which often results in invalidation.
5. People are afraid to risk looking like a fool, worse yet, being called a racist.
6. We've been socialized not to talk about race. This leads to colorblind ideology creating anxiety in noticing racial differences for fear of being seen as bad or racist.
7. Talking about race can elicit feelings of shame, blame, and guilt and feeds their resistance to grow.
8. Our identities are tied in to our assumptions, attitudes, and beliefs. When people are resistant, they are not just defending their point of view, they are also protecting their identity.
9. What is not said is often more important than what is said—and more difficult to bring out.
10. Race is an emotionally laden topic and you are an emotionally invested facilitator.

## ASSESSING YOUR FACILITATION STYLE

Awareness of your own cultural norms and styles of engaging can help you to become a more effective facilitator. Be conscious and flexible in your approach. Facilitators who can use different modalities are more likely to reach diverse audiences. This is particularly important when someone else's style of communication bumps up against your own. You should also recognize the dominant cultural style of communicating, not judging one as inherently superior or inferior. For example, if you predominately think in a linear fashion, that style is seen as "normal" and is overvalued in the United States. You will have to work harder to listen to and understand someone who is more circular or who uses stories and metaphors to make their point. The styles listed on the left of the column tend to be dominant cultural norms.

**Make an X along the line to indicate your style.**

| | |
|---|---|
| I avoid conflict | I embrace conflict |
| I'm a nonverbal processor | I'm a verbal processor |
| I stick to the agenda | I'm flexible with agendas |
| I hide emotion | I speak with emotion |
| I make points in a linear fashion | I make points through stories (circular) |
| I'm mostly still | I gesture frequently |
| I like a lot of personal space | I like close proximity and touch |
| I like facts and figures to teach | I use stories to teach |
| I stand in one place | I move around the room |

What else do you notice about your style of facilitating?

_____

_____

_____

_____

# Chapter Nine

## Basic Facilitation Tips

It is not our differences that divide us. It is our inability to recognize, accept and celebrate those differences.

—Audre Lorde

*Don't expect that everyone in the room will shift, but know that at the very least you can plant seeds that can eventually lead to change.*

Facilitating is different from training, in that it requires you to effectively navigate the dynamics of complex relationships, whereas training focuses on developing a new set of skills, such as learning how to use new software. Learning to facilitate effectively is a process that requires a great deal of patience and practice. Whether you are facilitating a workshop on something as complex and challenging as race relations or delivering a "how to" training, there are some basic strategies you can add to your toolkit that will help you achieve positive results.

Focus on learning one or two new skills at a time, rather than trying to change many habits at once. Practice until it becomes second nature, then try another. After your workshop, debrief your successes and challenges by talking with a colleague or by journaling. This way, you can track your progress and celebrate small steps you might otherwise miss. This also enables you to identify patterns in your behaviors that create barriers you might not otherwise be aware of.

It is not uncommon for facilitators to experience some physiological effects from presenting information and engaging participants in deep dialogue. No matter how well the workshop goes, it is normal to experience fatigue or "a low" afterwards because of the mental labor and adrenaline used. Although we always have participants evaluate our workshops so we can grow our skills, immediately following the workshop may not be the best time to review critical feedback. Talking through what you thought you did well and identifying areas that you need to improve on before soliciting feedback from others makes it easier to be open to critique.

The important thing to remember is that everyone starts somewhere and that it takes time and practice to get better. Give yourself grace, learn from your mistakes, and keep pushing. You can't control everything or everyone, nor will you ever be prepared to handle every situation that comes your way. No matter how good you are at leading the conversation, some participants may still walk away feeling resistant.

## 1. **Practice**

Even after you've learned a new strategy, there can be a tendency to go back to your old habits, especially in stressful situations. One of the best ways to actually shift your behaviors is to role-play a variety of common scenarios. We encourage you to practice facilitating difficult conversations as a way to learn effective responses. Trying it out with a colleague gives you a safe place to learn from your mistakes. You can also benefit from practicing how to effectively engage with people you will come across in everyday situations who make offensive remarks or push your hot buttons.

## 2. **Don't Take Participants' Negative Responses and Reactions Personally**

Your participants bring with them different attitudes, beliefs, and experiences around race relations. Try not to take their responses and reactions to heart. Participants often blame the facilitator, making you the object of their anger rather than looking inward at themselves. This is easy to do when feeling defensive about a topic, such as unearned privilege, that elicits shame and guilt. Knowing that some participants will resist changing their beliefs and that it is not unusual for them to project their issues onto you as a way to avoid critically reflecting can help ease your discomfort. When you take it personally, you are more likely to become defensive or respond in ways that move participants further away from your goals.

We realize that saying, "Don't take it personally," is easier said than done. Here's one strategy we sometimes visualize in these moments. Hold your hand out in front of you, palm side up. Imagine someone throwing an angry comment aimed at you. Now catch it. Don't let it hit you in your heart where it hurts the most. Now look at it in the palm of your hand and try to imagine what might be going on for that person to cause their response. Are they afraid? Have they had past negative experiences? What are they protecting themselves from? What might really be going on underneath their words? This type of thinking will help you begin to develop questions to ask the participant rather than simply react to what they say. As you get more practice with this strategy, you will be able to respond in ways that lead to growth rather than further defensiveness.

## 3. **Approach with a Positive Attitude Rather Than a Defensive One**

You may have heard about a "difficult" participant before meeting them or got a negative impression about someone from a brief interaction. It could be that they remind you of someone who has pushed your buttons in the past. For example, we've had experiences in workshops with older white men acting in oppressive ways. In these instances, we seek out their forgiveness, viewing them as potential allies rather than enemies. Whatever the case, it's natural to feel disconnected from some of your participants and in some instances find yourself disliking them. It is important that you are aware of your bias and assumptions and make a concerted effort to find the good in these particular people in hopes of moving beyond your initial impression. One strategy is to take a breath and envision that person as someone you care about who believes in justice but who doesn't yet see injustice in the same ways that you do.

### 4. **Modify Your Workshop at Any Given Moment**

Even if you've facilitated an activity a hundred times, it can be difficult to know exactly how long it will take. It often depends on the audience and what comes up in the dialogue. Be prepared to modify your agenda at any given moment to meet the needs of your audience. We think of activities as stimuli used for the purpose of getting courageous conversations started. Sometimes the conversation that is occurring in the room is bringing about the very thing you wanted to have happen, without need for the activity. Following are some ideas for modifying your agenda:

- *Meet them where they're at.* Listen for cues that indicate the level of understanding of the majority of participants in the group. Are you hearing denial or invalidation of racial experiences? Are people using terms such as "institutional racial privilege" or "internalized superiority," indicating a deeper level of understanding? Based on their cues, change the language and examples you use to meet them where they're at. For example, with some groups we may say "unearned advantages," rather than "white privilege" early in the presentation and then shift the language to white privilege as they develop understanding. When we realize our participants have more depth and knowledge of the topic, we'll talk directly about white supremacy culture early on.

- *Bring a few extra activities.* We've gone into workshops intending to focus on skill development and quickly realized the group needed to do more awareness work before they could develop the types of skills we had planned to teach them. Bring a few different activities just in case you need to switch up.

- *Allow participants to continue the conversation.* When the conversation at tables or during whole group discussion is rich and meaningful and the learning you had hoped for is occurring, continue the conversation even though the allotted time for that section is up. Instead, shorten the time planned for another activity or take something off of the agenda altogether, such as a video clip you were going to show.

    Sometimes an activity will take longer than you planned, or the richness of the conversation has you doubting if what you had planned is the best next step. You can ask the group what they would like to do when you aren't quite sure what would benefit them the most. Tell them what would get removed from the agenda, and ask them if they would prefer to stop and move on or continue doing what they're doing. Try not to waste too much time explaining and have them decide. Think through how you will ask them, and have them quickly do a show of hands. There are other times when you will make the decision yourself without informing them or including them in the process.

- *When a new topic is introduced.* If an issue outside of your agenda comes up that feels relevant, one strategy is to ask the group if that is something they'd like time to process. Asking for a show of hands for who would like to talk about what came up usually works. However, don't assume this is a concern of the whole group just because it is raised by a few people. You may find time later for small group discussions on that topic. If participants decide not to go that route, remind them of the norm "Accept and Expect Nonclosure." The conversation can and will continue in other ways in the future.

- *When one participant is resistant.* A few participants may want to engage with someone who is resistant. Try to balance the needs of the entire group with the needs of one or two. There have been occasions when we've spent too much time focused on one person, while the rest of the group was ready to move on. In these situations you risk losing the majority of the group. This is particularly problematic when the needs of one or two people end up dominating the needs of the majority. This is an example of how white privilege can sometimes be reinforced even in workshops addressing racism.

- *Take a break.* When you realize you need to change the agenda, sit down for a moment while they are engaging at their tables or give the group a short break so you can pull your ideas together and readjust the agenda.

- *When you're getting in the way.* Recognize where your need for control or security is getting in the way of the needs of the group. If you've spent a lot of time planning what you thought was a great agenda, you may be reluctant to change direction, even when you see it's what the group needs. There is greater risk when following the group into unplanned territory, but sometimes it is necessary. Avoid letting your fear of diving into the unknown keep you from doing what's in the best interest of the group. Be willing to take risks and experience discomfort. There will be times when this will work out beautifully and other times when it won't go so well. In either case, you will learn from the experience and become a better facilitator as a result

## 5. Get Participants Back on Track

Participants want and expect you to take control of the conversations. Think about how many times you have been in a workshop of any sort and one person dominated the conversation or was constantly off topic. Did you roll your eyes? Did your mind wander? Did you sigh? Or maybe you had internal dialogue thinking, "When is the facilitator going to do something about this?" However you reacted, it is likely that you didn't have a lot of patience for the facilitator or the person speaking. Remember that participants are there for a reason, and when they feel the conversation is no longer relevant or is moving away from the objectives, they will become disengaged and hold you responsible for the results. Don't frustrate your participants by being too flexible—take control! Being a facilitator means you are going to have to become comfortable with redirecting participants to keep them on topic.

We've had people tell us after the fact that they were going to walk out of our workshop if we hadn't stopped someone from dominating the conversation. As a facilitator you have to walk your talk or you run the risk of losing credibility. Some of the core principles of courageous conversations are embedded in the norms. It's important that you model those norms by taking risks and experiencing your own discomfort. The following are some helpful tips for getting participants back on topic:

- *Enroll the help of your participants up front.* Ask them to be conscious of the amount of airtime they take up in large and small group conversations. Encourage them to listen if they're usually the first to talk and to take risks to engage if they tend to hold back. Remind participants to leave room for silence while people gather their thoughts and build up the courage to speak in front of a large audience. Share your own style of engaging as an example of why it's important to create the space. Remind them that, as a part of the learning community, they can speak up if they feel the conversation is off topic.

- *When participants get off topic.* Pay attention to nonverbal cues from your participants, such as looking down or away, shifting in their seats looking at their phones, sidebar conversations, and other indicators that they have become disengaged. It can mean it's time to interrupt. Also, trust your own internal voice. Are you losing interest in what the participant is saying? If you are becoming bored or disengaged, it is highly likely that others are too.

- *Allow for differences in communication styles.* Be careful not to perpetuate racism by accepting only one way of communicating. Some people tell a story to make their point or need time to process out loud. Give it a little time so you can assess the situation before you interrupt. If the person takes a long time, you may want to add a few key points to get everyone back and engaged.

- *Move in closer.* When you begin to sense that a participant is taking up too much air-time, slowly move in closer. If you have established credibility and rapport with your participants, putting a hand on their shoulder can be an acceptable way to signal it's time to move on.

- *Use the "parking lot" strategy.* Acknowledge that what they are talking about is not planned on the agenda but that it is an important topic. Tell them you will write their idea down on poster paper labeled "Parking Lot," and if there is enough time at the end, address it. This validates that what they shared and at the same time recognizes that it's important to continue for the sake of time.

- *If what they share is something you plan to address later.* When a participant brings up a topic that you plan to talk about later, tell them, "I plan to cover that later on in the day, if I don't remember to bring it up, will you please remind me?"

- *When your culture conflicts with interrupting.* For some cultures, interrupting is considered rude or disrespectful. For example, interrupting your elders might be something that is socially unacceptable. When this is the case, talk openly about it. For example, before interrupting you might say something like this: "This is really difficult for me, my grandmother would scold me for this, but I'm going to have to interrupt you so we can move on to the next part of the workshop, Mr. Lau."

- *Validate what was said.* Use statements that leave the person feeling heard and understood, and at the same time remind them of your goal.
  - *Sexism is also a very important topic. Today we are going to keep the conversation focused on race and racism. How are those two connected?*
  - *I would love to hear more of your thoughts about that. However, we still have a lot of information and activities to cover. Why don't you see me after this session?*
  - *What you are bringing up could be an entire session and would take up much more time than we have right now, but it's a topic worthy of discussion at some other time.*
  - *I wish we had more time to explore that issue; however, there's so much we still have to cover.*

> • *I hate to stop you in the middle of what you're saying, but I'm concerned about the time. I apologize, but we have to move on.*
> • *I'd be happy to talk with you further about that during the break, but we're going to have to get back on topic and move on.*

There have been occasions when participants have become angry or defensive when they're interrupted or redirected, but for the most part participants realize when they're getting off topic and will laugh about it or apologize when it is called to their attention. Keeping participants on track is a necessary facilitation skill that, if well developed, will benefit everyone in the room.

## 6. Keep in Mind that Learning Occurs Differently, at Different Times, for Different People

Everyone is at different places on the continuum of cultural competence. What works for one person may not work for another. Remember that change happens over time. Sometimes you have to settle for just planting seeds of new ideas and thinking. What grows from your efforts may occur long after the workshop. I recently taught a multicultural perspectives course. On the last day, when students were given time to process their overall experiences of the class, one of my white students shared that her boyfriend, who was also white, had been trying to talk with her for years about race and social justice issues. She had been very resistant to learning or moving beyond her own limited understanding. She stated that because of this class, she was finally beginning to share his understanding, and, as a result, they were engaging in deep meaningful conversations. I believe that if it weren't for her boyfriend previously trying to engage her in conversation, she would have come to class with a different mind-set. Her boyfriend tilled the soil and planted the seeds so that she was ready to grow by the time she entered the class.

- *People vary in their understanding.* An effective facilitator keeps this at the forefront of their thinking. They understand that people are at different levels of their racial/ethnic identity development.[1] Just because someone belongs to a specific racial group does not mean they think the same way about race issues. For example, some African Americans will believe that race doesn't matter, others will see all white people as bad, and then there are those who have a perspective somewhere in the middle. As a skilled facilitator, try to meet participants where they are, not where you think they should be. For example, someone who is deeply invested in individualism and color blindness will likely not understand why providing different opportunities based on skin color is necessary. You'll need to ask questions or engage them in activities to help them see how race matters.

- *You won't shift everyone's thinking.* Not everyone will be open to changing their attitudes or beliefs, no matter how skilled you are at facilitating. Learn to accept this.

## 7. Show Understanding to White Participants Struggling with Their Own Oppression

There are many groups who suffer from experiences of oppression. Some white participants will be dealing with their own unresolved brokenness and won't have the mental or emotional space to learn about the impact of racial oppression. See them as human and give them grace.

---

1 To learn more about racial/ethnic identity development models, see chapters 11 and 12 in *Counseling the Culturally Diverse: Theory and Practice* by Derald Wing Sue and David Sue (2013).

We're not talking about the times people insert their own experiences to avoid the discomfort of having conversations about race. Rather, we've worked with people whose pain is so real and deep they don't have the capacity to deal with the pain of another at this time in their lives. It is not uncommon in these situations for the participant to approach you during a break and tell you about their own struggles.

An example of this might be a participant who is dealing with identity issues around their sexual orientation. If this is something they have not fully embraced as a result of their own oppressive experiences, it will be hard for them to set this aside. As best you can, honor their brokenness while at the same time keeping the large group focusing on race. All issues of power, privilege, and oppression should be addressed, but there are too many issues to try to discuss them all within a half-day or full-day workshop. You might say something like this:

> *Thank you for taking the risk to share with us your own painful experiences of oppression. It sounds like you are really grappling with some similar issues like the ones we are talking about today. It makes sense that you would struggle with engaging in conversations around race when your own experiences of oppression are so close to the surface and unresolved. I want to honor where you are at in this work and the pain that is caused from your own experiences of oppression, but at the same time I will need to keep our group focused on race. Does this make sense? I hope you will do the necessary work to address your own needs so that someday we can be allies in this work.*

When we have accurately assessed that the person is not trying to derail the conversation about race, we find that participants understand and at the same time feel heard. You can use this new knowledge of who is in the room to broaden your examples or make connections to race with other forms of oppression. Talking about the intersections of our identities is more inclusive than asking someone to ignore one part of self in order to focus on other.

### 8. Be Yourself. Don't Try to Emulate Someone Else's Facilitation Style

You probably found yourself on at least one occasion thinking, "How do they do that!?" while hearing a presenter speak. Maybe you were amazed by their skill and ability to draw audiences in. There are many different facilitation styles that work to engage participants. For example, some facilitators are able to stand behind the podium and capture most everyone's attention the entire time. That's not our style. We like to move around, weaving ourselves throughout the audience as we speak. While we have similarities, we also have our unique differences. Rather than try to emulate someone else, figure out what comes natural to you and discover your own style. This will be cultivated over time as you figure out what your audience does and does not respond to.

### 9. Clarify with Questions and Paraphrasing

Far too often conflict arises because what we think the person is saying and what they are actually saying are two different things. Another reason is that we jump to conclusions about why we think they said what they did. This can lead you down a path that could have been avoided had you asked clarifying questions or paraphrased. Rather than spending 2 or 3 minutes on a comment, you end up spending 5 to 10 because there is an entirely different topic put on the table for discussion. If there is any doubt or confusion about what the participant is saying, take a moment to clarify by asking questions or paraphrasing so they can confirm that your interpretation is accurate. Circle back around to the participant who originally made the comment to check for understanding. If you got it wrong, you might get a response like this:

"That's helpful, but it wasn't actually what I was saying. I was trying to say _____." Here are a few simple strategies:

- *I'm not sure I understand. Can you tell me more about that?*
- *Tell me if I'm not saying this right, but what I hear you saying is _____. Is that correct?*
- *Please tell me if I'm understanding you correctly, you're asking if _____. or You're saying that _____.*
- *(Ask permission) If I may paraphrase what you said, I'm hearing that you are concerned about _____. Did I capture your thoughts accurately?*
- *Give me pushback if I'm not accurately conveying your thoughts. I hear you saying _____.*
- *Correct me if I'm wrong, but you're essentially saying _____.*
- *I may only be 70 percent correct, but I think you are saying that _____.*
- *Let me see if I'm hearing you correctly. You want to know if _____.*
- *Can you say more?*
- *Tell me what you mean by _____.* (Restate a word or sentence they used.)

While clarifying or paraphrasing can be a useful tool, we want to make a note of caution. White facilitators using this strategy run the risk of perpetuating a perception of white superiority, and of people of color as inferior, particularly. This is connected to the experience that people of color have had in this country that when a white person says something, it is perceived as being better articulated, understood, or accepted. In other words, it wasn't understood until a white person said it. We are not suggesting white facilitators avoid using this strategy, but rather that they be mindful of the possible impact. If someone is offended by your questions or paraphrasing, show that you understand rather than try to prove it wasn't what you were doing or unconsciously thinking. Your openness to hearing their experience of you in that moment validates all of the times it has occurred for them. You can be a vehicle for them to process these very real experiences. What happens as a result is like magic. Your openness to hearing them name you as the perpetrator actually shows them that you are different from the people they have experienced in the past, resulting in them often recognizing that in this case they were wrong. It's when you try to explain or prove your innocence that you confirm your own guilt of being who they accuse you to be.

### 10. **Reframe**

Reframing is a well-known psychology term usually referred to as *cognitive reframing.* Wikipedia defines it as "changing the way people see things and trying to find alternative ways of viewing ideas, events, situations, or a variety of other concepts." As a facilitator you will often find yourself needing to provide an alternative perspective. In most cases, we invite other participants into the conversation to share their perspectives rather than engaging one-on-one with the participant who made the comment.

In essence, the entire workshop is meant to get participants to see things more broadly. Reframing is not going to change their thinking instantaneously, but it can help to shape the conversation so that participants, at the very least, are entertaining the idea that maybe the worldview they hold is not completely accurate. Below are a few examples of reframing statements made by participants:

*Joshua, you said you felt like conversations about white privilege always make you out to be an evil person because you're a white man who benefits from privileges you never asked for. It is very common for us to think of racism and privilege in terms of being good or bad people.*

*But we've found this dichotomy isn't very helpful for working together for social justice. How is it possible to benefit from white privilege* and *be a good person?*

*Ingrid, you said you have stopped looking to people of color for validation as a white ally and now are looking to white people for that support. Can I offer another way to look at it? (She agrees.) What if you were to look within yourself for the strength to continue this work, even without other people telling you you're doing a good job. What would you need to make that shift?*

*Huoy, I'm hearing you say race plays a much larger role in your life than any other identity. A lot of people feel like they have to rank what is most and least important. Instead of putting one above another, I'm wondering how you see race intersecting with your other identities? How are your class experiences related to race? Sexual orientation?*

Courage is the art of being the only one who knows you're scared to death.

—Harold Wilson

## STOP AND REFLECT

1. What is your greatest strength as a facilitator?
2. What is one goal you have to improve your facilitation? What are some small steps you can take to meet this goal?

_____

_____

_____

_____

_____

_____

_____

_____

# Chapter Ten

## Facilitation Strategies

While dealing with the content issues—for example, those defining racism or exploring institutional racism—the facilitator must also be aware of the process issues—how people are feeling, how they respond to one another, and so on.

—Judith H. Katz

### FACILITATION STRATEGIES

*Remember how much processing you did to deepen your understanding? Participants need time to process too!*

Gone are the days when professionals can stand up in front of an audience, stand behind a podium, and lecture for hours at a time. We now have enough understanding of how people learn to know that differentiating our instruction is necessary in order to meet the diverse learning styles of our audience. This is true for both youth and adult learning. One important way to do this is to provide learners the opportunity to process the information by talking about it and practicing new skills.

**People Remember ...**
**10%** *of what they* **READ**
**20%** *of what they* **HEAR**
**30%** *of what they* **SEE**
**50%** *of what they* **SEE** *and* **HEAR**
**70%** *of what they* **SAY** *and* **WRITE**
**90%** *of what they* **SAY** *as they* **DO**

*Source: David A. Sousa, How the Brain Learns (Virginia NASSP, 1995).*

It's not uncommon to teach the same way you were taught, so if you were a victim of "sit and get" type learning, it's going to require conscious practice to change these habits. The primary focus in this section is to shift from being "the" expert who has all the knowledge to the role of facilitator, where participants learn from you and from one another. Following are helpful strategies for facilitating adult learning on any topic:

### 1. **Give Participants Time to Process**

In order for participants to retain the information, you will need to provide them with the opportunity to discuss with others what they just experienced or heard. One way to do this is to allow time for reflection, after about every 10 minutes of lecture. This may not always be possible, but giving them just 2 minutes to reflect can make a difference. The more opportunities you provide, the more likely they will retain the information.

- *Stop and Jot.* This is an effective strategy when you have a lot of information to share and don't have time for long processing breaks. It allows participants a moment to reflect on what they've just heard, with little interruption in your presentation. Ask participants to take a moment to jot down a few notes—for example, about what they would like to remember, something that stands out for them, or reactions to what was said.

- *Small breakout sessions.* Have participants talk at their tables in small groups. This is a great way for participants to think about an issue collectively and to hear different perspectives on a given subject. Have participants seated in groups of 4 to 8 and give them specific questions to discuss. Provide them enough time to engage so everyone who wants to share can. Anywhere from 10 to 20 minutes is usually sufficient, depending on the topic and how many people are in each group.

- *Large/Whole group discussions.* Large, or whole group, discussions are opportunities to enter into discourse with the entire room. We utilize them as a way to hear what is coming up for participants. Sometimes we will have them respond to prompts and record their responses on poster paper. Other times we will invite a few participants in the room to share aloud what they discussed in their groups. It all depends on the amount of time we have and our objectives for the day. We'll also ask individuals in the room their thoughts, feelings, comments, or experiences on a lecture or activity we just experienced together. Whole group discussions provide the facilitator with the opportunity to make comments, clarify, provide input, and shape thinking.

- *Think-Pair-Share.* This strategy is particularly helpful when you want them to reflect on questions that require a level of vulnerability they might not expose in a larger setting. It offers them a chance to explore their thoughts, feelings, and stories with one other person, with relatively low risk involved. We plan think-pair-shares throughout our agenda but occasionally will use them spontaneously after we've asked the whole group a question, and no one responds. This may be an indicator the question is either too risky to respond to in the presence of such a large group or participants need more time to think about it. Once they have shared with a partner, reintroduce the question to the entire group. This will almost always result in large group participation. With this approach, a measure of safety is provided so they can test their thinking without fearing an entire room of people will judge them.

  Below is how think-pair-share works. Instructions can be simply stated by saying, "Take 2 minutes to think about _____, then partner with the person next to you and share your thoughts and feelings."

**THINK** ➔ Take 2 min-
utes to think
individually and
write about
your thoughts
and feelings.

**PAIR** ➔ Take 4 min-
utes each to
share your re-
flections with
a partner.

**SHARE** ➔ Large/Whole
group sharing

- *Silence*. How does silence make you feel? If it makes you uneasy, you will need to work on becoming comfortable with the discomfort. There are several situations when silence commonly occurs when facilitating.

  a. ***When something significant happens.*** Often the emotion comes from a person of color who is experiencing the impact of racism through the activity or the retelling of a story. This is a time to call for silence and just be present in the moment. If someone jumps in to speak, thoughtfully stop them and suggest everyone sit with what was just experienced. We may add something to the effect of: "Listening is a form of action." This type of silence honors the story of another. After the silence, check back in with the participant who shared and see if there is anything else they would like to add. When you sense the room is ready to continue, circle back around and invite those who jumped in to share. This approach is commonly used when a person of color is crying and a white person jumps in, usually out of deep feelings of guilt and shame, wanting to make everything better.

  b. ***When a question is asked and no one responds.*** Silence that occurs after you ask a question can feel awkward. Your response depends on whether participants are taking the time to reflect on your question, don't understand the question, or if they are not responding right away because they are uncomfortable with the question. This will be difficult to determine. If you think the former is true, give them the time to reflect on the question or restate it in a different way. If you think the latter is true, after a moment of silence remind them of the norm to take risks and experience discomfort. You can also have them engage in a think-pair-share. In either case, allow at least 40 to 50 seconds of silence before interrupting. Resist the temptation to ask another question or to fill in the silence with your words. This can feel like a long time, but we find that more often than not, someone will eventually speak up to get the conversation going. If someone in the room speaks up who has already spoken a lot, ask the person to hold on for a moment to give others a chance to respond. It may be that they are uncomfortable with the silence, too, or they believe no one else wants to share, when, in reality, others may just need more time to think or become comfortable with their discomfort.

  c. ***When you're not sure what to say or do.*** This is the most challenging type of silence you will struggle with. It's when something has happened or occurred in the room and you are stuck. How do you proceed to get the room unstuck? Though the silence may last a short time, it usually feels like an eternity. Your mind will be racing as you try to figure out what to do or say next. You will feel a lot of pressure to have the answers, and that pressure you place on yourself can immobilize you. A couple of suggestions: if you have built enough credibility with participants, it may work to tell them you are stuck. For example, I was once teaching a class on race at a Christian college. The conversation got extremely heated about the topic of sexual orientation. I facilitated it as best I could and for as long as I could, but when I got to the point of not knowing what to do next, I told them I was stuck with where to go with the conversation. I then told them to get in a large circle and hold hands, and I led the entire class in prayer. This was more than acceptable for this setting, but I had never led one person in prayer let alone a group of 90 people. This will rarely if ever be an option for you given the public settings you are likely to be facilitating these conversations in, but our point is to give you an example of ways in which we have announced to the group we are at a loss of what to do. Other solutions are to allow for the silence and to call for a break to give yourself a chance to think about how to proceed, even though you risk losing the momentum that was occurring in the moment. We also mention strategies later in this book for how to invite other participants into the dialogue so their thoughts, feelings, and expertise become a part of the dialogue and it's not all on your shoulders.

- *1-1-1 Reflection.* This particular reflection is something that works well at the close of the day. A colleague of ours, Anita Morales, taught us to use these questions: (1) What's one thing you learned today? (2) What's one thing you will do differently as a result of what you learned? (3) What's one question, concern, or fear you have? After participants are given enough time to write out their responses, have them either pair-share or discuss their responses at their tables. We will usually follow this with a whole group discussion, inviting 2 to 4 people to each share one of their responses. Again, how many people we have share in large group discussion always depends on how much time is remaining.

## 2. **Bring Everyone Back Together**

Sometimes it can be challenging to bring everyone back together once they've become engaged in conversation or are returning from a break. It's important you do not begin until you have everyone's attention. This is another strategy that helps you build credibility. If you start the lesson and people are not seated or are continuing to talk, it can be because they have not yet realized you want their attention or they are so engaged in their conversation that they choose to continue talking. Though usually not intended, it can come across as disrespectful. Use your facilitator voice and speak loudly so everyone can hear. We find the following strategies helpful.

- State loudly, "Let's come back together as a whole group."
- When time is almost up for pair-share dialogue, prepare them by stating, "If you haven't switched partners by now, please do so."
- "30 seconds left. Wrap up what you are saying, please."
- Project a timer on the screen so everyone can keep track of time.
- Begin to start the next topic of conversation, and then pause to let everyone know you will wait until everyone is ready. Usually, participants will ask their colleagues who are still talking to stop because they are eager to get started.
- Establish a signal for attention (raising hand, chimes, lights off, etc.) at the start of the discussions.
- Ask someone in the room if their organization has a way of bringing everyone back together. Sometimes participants will volunteer this information when they see you are struggling to get everyone's attention. When this is the case, use what works for them.

- At the start of the activity, have each group select a volunteer to be the timekeeper.
- Thoughtfully ask the few people who are still talking to come back together with the entire group; for example, "Laura, are you ready? We are ready to get started."
- Use humor and start calling out names of people who are ready: "I see that Melissa is ready to get started. Thank you, Melissa. I see that Regina is ready to get started. Thank you, Regina. I see that Melony's table is ready." Usually you only need to mention a couple of names for everyone to come together as a group.

### 3. Utilize a Variety of Teaching Strategies

There are many different learning styles, including visual, musical, intrapersonal and kinesthetic. Changing the way you teach the content throughout the day helps to reach a wider audience of learners.

- Utilize a combination of video clips, small group discussions, think-pair-share, interactive activities, articles, lecture, role play, and other methods of engaging.

- After you've outlined your agenda, look back to see if you've alternated between different learning modalities. You may want to change the order of your activities to balance out the learning modalities.

- Think about the flow of the day. Plan the bulk of your lecture or content information in the morning. After lunch, keep people moving and engaging with one another as much as possible. Try to avoid deep-thinking exercises for the last hour of the day when participants are most tired.

### 4. Limit Questions That Seek "Correct" Answers

If you have information you want to share, don't make participants play the "Guess what's in my head" or "Who knows the correct answer" game. Give them the information up front and then ask them open-ended questions so they can make meaning of it based on their experiences. It's embarrassing to be asked a question and volunteer the answer only to be told you are wrong. When a facilitator asks a question that clearly has a correct answer, we are less likely to raise our hands, unless we are certain we know the right response. Courageous conversations are about engaging. It's not about figuring out who has the most experience talking about race. So if you want participants to engage, ask them questions that invite them to explore.

For example, asking participants, "Who knows what cultural competence means?" conveys there is a correct answer. However, changing the question slightly to "What does cultural competence mean to you?" allows more participants to feel they have something to contribute, and therefore they are more likely to engage as you add to the knowledge. Here are some strategies for facilitating open dialogue that encourage learning together in community:

- When someone is close to correctly explaining an idea, but there is more to be said, thank them for what they did share, and then ask, "Can anyone build on what Jessie just shared?"

- If someone answers a question with a few words or one sentence, encourage them to expand by saying, "Can you say more about that?"

- When someone says something that contains language or words that could easily be misunderstood, saying, "Tell us what you mean by _____," helps bring clarity.

- When someone gives a response that you don't want others to accept as part of the definition, acknowledge it's not how you understand the definition without shaming them. For example, you could say, "I have never thought about it that way before." Refer to the experts by adding, "Sue and Sue don't include that in their definition, but it's an interesting way to think about it."

- When someone gives a good response but it needs to be stated more clearly for other participants in the room, have them restate it in a different way or ask, "Would you mind if I reworded what you just said to help you make your point?"

## 5. Engage Participants Who Have Not Spoken

It's not uncommon for a few participants to dominate the conversation. A successful workshop has the majority of participants engaged through both critical reflection and group discussions. However, not everyone is comfortable talking in large group settings. Their anxiety and fears are likely to be heightened, given that the conversation is about race. One strategy that you will need to be careful with is calling on someone who has not volunteered to share his or her thoughts, opinions, experiences, or feelings. This can be an effective strategy for bringing more voices into the room, when done well. It's also a clever way to keep everyone attentive, because participants won't know if or when they will be called on. But for some this approach will increase anxiety, and for others it will feel like an invitation to open up and join in. Building rapport, understanding cultural communication differences, and a willingness to take risks will help you navigate this strategy in a way that doesn't leave participants feeling put on the spot or embarrassed. Following are helpful tips for getting more participation from quieter voices in the room:

- *I'd like to hear from someone I haven't had the opportunity to hear from yet.*
- *Let's hear from some different voices in the room.*
- *I'd love to hear your voice today, Linda. What are your thoughts about ____?*
- *Chanel, would you be open to sharing your thoughts about ____?*
- *Would anyone who hasn't had a chance to share like to respond?*
- *Dan, we haven't had a chance to hear from you; what are your thoughts about ____?*

If you call on a participant by name and they don't respond right away, give them a moment. If it appears that they are uneasy or are really struggling, let them off the hook by calling on someone else.

Avoid calling on the participants of color in the room to be the experts of their group or to represent their group's experience. They are there to learn just like everyone else.

## 6. Respond to What Isn't Being Said

Sometimes participants will ask questions or make statements that don't speak to their real concerns or opinions. For example, in one workshop we had a man ask a question about the intersection of Marxist beliefs and white privilege. As we looked at each other in confusion, I turned to him and said, "I have a thought about that. I think when someone asks a question like that it is usually because they have their own opinion. What are your thoughts about it?" We were able to share a laugh, and sure enough, he had a theory he wanted to share with the group.

At other times, someone may be commenting on racial dynamics without wanting to say it directly. This is usually the case with people of color in a setting where they don't feel safe speaking their opinions directly. In this situation, you may try to guess what their question is really about as you answer. It can also work to respond with a question.

In one session, the sole black person in the room asked why I had started the workshop with a video by a light-skinned black man. I had a feeling that she was concerned with a white facilitator talking about racism, and part of her question was about centering whiteness in the discussion. I responded first by asking her about this, but she became upset that I responded to her question with a question. So I backed up, explained my decision, and talked about where I was coming from as a white facilitator. Then I asked her if she was concerned about the predominance of white perspectives. She engaged with me at that point, and we were able to model for other participants in the room how tricky and multilayered these conversations are.

### 7. **Take a Pulse of the Situation**

Taking a pulse of the situation is based on of the work of Kathy Obear, who says we need to reflect on how the process is going as a group. When things are not going well or you sense that people are not working in community with one another in a way that helps to bridge the racial divide—stop—and have participants take a pulse of the situation by reflecting on the process. Having conversations about race should be a liberating experiencing, not an oppressing one. Stopping the conversation and having them talk about how they are treating one another is a great way to redirect to more effective ways of engaging.

- *What do you notice happening right now?*
- *How are we working together in this moment?*
- *How well are we respecting each other?*
- *How would you describe how we are treating one another?*
- *Courageous conversations are about truth and reconciliation. In what ways are we speaking our truth that can lead us to reconciliation, and what do we need to do differently?*

### 8. **Walk Around during Small Group Discussions**

Participants are more likely to talk openly in small groups than in whole group conversations. Walk around and listen to the conversation so you can gain insight into their thoughts, feelings, attitudes, and beliefs. This can help you prepare to respond to comments and think through what you will say when bringing the groups back together for large group discussion. If you want to address something you heard said in small groups, and the person who said it will obviously know you are referring to their comment, ask their permission.

*There was some great dialogue happening when I was walking around. I heard people talking about feeling angry that their organization is not engaging in these conversations and someone mentioned_____. You would then add your thoughts and comments.*

*This table was having an interesting discussion about institutional privilege. Would someone from the group mind sharing what you talked about?*

*I heard you telling a really powerful story, Andrea, and I'm wondering if you wouldn't mind sharing it with the entire group.*

- *Notice group dynamics.* Pay particular attention to group dynamics during interactive activities, such as when participants are laughing during activities that bring about discomfort, a few participants are dominating the conversation, or when people are not participating at all. You can use your observations to engage large group discussions or within the smaller groups. When engaging the small group, so as not to take up their discussion time, ask a few questions of the group and then walk away.

### *Addressing Small Groups*

- When you've circled around the room a second or third time and find that the same participants are still speaking: *We only have about 5 minutes left. If there are people at your table who have not spoken, be sure to leave room for them to process their learning. You may need to invite them in.*
- *Has everyone at your table had a chance to share?*
- *What are some of the group dynamics you are noticing at your table?*

  - *Don't take over the small group conversations.* Participants have a tendency to want to pull you in to their table conversation, or you may feel the urge to comment on something that was said. While it's okay to join them in discussion, be careful not to dominate the conversation and take away the little bit of time they have to process. Simply stating, "I'm here to just listen" can help redirect the focus back to them.

  - *When you see a group getting off track.* When participants derail the conversation, don't hesitate to insert yourself into the discussion and bring it back on task. This isn't always easy to do. Sometimes just standing at their table for a minute or two can be a gentle reminder. However, there will be occasions when you will need to verbally redirect them.

- *Has everyone had an opportunity to share their thoughts about _____?*
- *We have about 5 minutes left. Where are you at in the discussion?*
- *Remember the norm to stay engaged.*
- *Sounds like this discussion is triggering a lot of other experiences for you. You are going to need to wrap up in a few minutes. Are you ready?*
- *Have you finished processing the questions I've posted? If not, I want to make sure that you have the opportunity to do so.*

  - *Sit down with a group to listen and observe.* Rather than walking around and stopping at each table, actually sit down with each group for a period of time. If you run out of time and are unable to sit with every group, visit the others later in the day. This approach provides insight into how they are processing the information, offers you the opportunity to hear resistance that hasn't been voiced in the large group, allows you to hear from participants who haven't spoken so far, and furthers relationship building.

  - *A participant asks a question or makes a comment better addressed to the entire group.* This can happen while you are walking around to tables or when someone broke away from their group to seek you out. Sometimes they want to correct you on something you said or did earlier in the day and out of respect don't want to embarrass you in front of the entire group. It could also be they feel tentative about asking their question in front of the entire room. Rather than having one person benefit from your response, encourage the person to bring their question or comment up during the large group discussion if it applies to others so you can respond to it then. You may have to invite them to share their comments when the time comes rather than wait for them to feel comfortable enough to interject.

- *That's a great question, one that I would guess others also have. Would you be willing to bring that up when we come back together as a large group so everyone can benefit from the conversation?*

- *Sean, you asked a great question during the break. Would you mind sharing it with the group?*
- *Tammy, you took a risk and shared with me something that I had not previously been aware of regarding language I used that might be seen as offensive. I learned something new. Would you share?*
- *I get asked that question a lot. You reminded me that I need to address that. I'm going to wait to respond and share it with the larger group.*
- *Thank you, I didn't realize I was pronouncing "Muslim" wrong. Would you be willing to share the correct pronunciation with the entire group?*

Many participants will see you as having a level of expertise they don't have. As a result, they may feel what they have to share is inadequate in comparison or they fear being judged. This can cause them to feel reluctant to speak their truth with you in their presence. As you walk around, if you notice participants getting quiet or seeming uncomfortable when you approach, give them space by walking away or tell them you're just there to listen. This commonly occurs when participants are role-playing. They have a lot of anxiety about doing it right, and your presence can add to their fears. For this reason, we generally do not observe role-plays unless it appears participants are comfortable with us watching.

### Addressing the Whole Group
- *How many of you felt discomfort while engaging in this conversation? Would anyone be willing to talk about it?*
- *I heard a great deal of laughter during this activity, what was going on for some folks?*
- *We've been talking about color-blind ideology and reasons why it's important to notice race. I'm going to take a risk by saying I noticed white people were the first to talk in nearly every group. Let's talk about that.*

### 9. **Meet the Needs of Participants with Limited English**
Some participants who are multilingual, or for whom English is a second language, have difficulty keeping up with the conversation. As you are speaking, participants who are multilingual maybe translating in their heads what you are saying to their native language. Of course, all of this depends on the individual and how long they have spoken English. Organizations providing culturally relevant professional development (CRPD) should provide translation services for staff members who do not speak English. Recommend and welcome these services when offered by a client. Here are some strategies for bridging the gap for English language learners:

- Give both verbal and written directions for activities.
- Check in with your participants who speak English as a second language individually to make sure they are clear on what is being asked.
- Be prepared to offer to partner with them if they appear uncomfortable with the pair-share activities.
- If you tend to talk fast, slow down.
- Refrain from calling on a person for whom English is their second language when they are not volunteering to speak. They may not be where you are in the discussion.
- When activities rely heavily on the written or spoken word, check in with them during break or during the written activity to see how they are doing. Invite their feedback on how you can improve the experience for them.
- Use visual cues, including images in slideshows to support understanding.

- Plan activities that don't rely heavily on verbal communication.
- Try to avoid difficult to translate idioms, such as "pet peeves," that are not crucial to your presentation.
- Encourage participants with a common home language to sit together and process in that language.
- If possible, provide them with handouts prior to the workshop so they have more time to look them over.

## STOP AND REFLECT

1. What are some facilitation strategies that you have used in your workshops?
2. Which strategies would you like to practice becoming skilled at?
3. Which behaviors do you need to work on avoiding?

# SECTION III

# RESPONDING TO TRIGGERS IN INTERCULTURAL CONFLICT

Our comfort zone includes all the things we have done often enough to feel comfortable doing. Any behavior outside our comfort zone can result in fear, guilt, worthlessness, hurt feelings, anger and discouragement.

—John Roger and Pete McWilliams

# Chapter Eleven

## Examining a Situation for Understanding

If you have come here to help me, you are wasting your time. But if you have come because your liberation is bound up with mine, then let us work together.

—Lilla Watson

*Knowledge without understanding is just as dangerous as understanding without knowledge.*

**M**ost of us can think of a time when we felt like the person we were talking to just didn't get it. No matter what we said or how we said it, they simply refused to see a different point of view. Sometimes when reflecting back on these conversations over the next several hours, or, if you're anything like us, over the next several months, we think, "If only I had said ____."

Unfortunately, there is no formula, no one right way to engage in conversations about racism, power, and privilege that will automatically bring others to another level of understanding. Having knowledge of racial/ethnic identity development can help you discern how to best approach the conversation. Even when you are able to use your understanding of racial/ethnic identity development to help pinpoint what stage you're in and what stage the person you are conversing with is in, it doesn't mean you will find the "magical" words needed to move them forward in their thinking.

What we can do is rethink how we approach conversations about race and practice strategies that invite people into the conversation rather than increase their defensiveness. Imagine yourself in the shoes of the person you were talking to. They were most likely just as frustrated with your lack of understanding as you were theirs. In fact, after you left, they probably thought, "If only I had said _____."

Real shifts in our identity require relationships, time, and a personal motivation to see the world in new ways in order to better understand others. Instead of coming up with the right thing to say, we would all benefit from developing active listening and critical questioning skills. It is not nearly as easy as venting or arguing, but what we should be saying to ourselves after the conversation is, "If only I had *asked* _____."

When you find yourself embroiled in a discussion about race, here are a few questions to ask yourself.

### 1. **Do I really care about this person?**

If you find yourself disliking the person you are talking with more and more with each breath, chances are no new learning is taking place for either of you. Weigh what you have invested in the relationship with the need to maintain your integrity. In other words, if this is a conversation that is likely to surface trauma, do you both have an investment in listening to each other in this place and time? Is this a case where the pain outweighs the gain? Once, after an exhaustive email conversation, I told someone I did not "agree to disagree," but, rather, I agreed to revisit the conversation in a different way in the future. The more I read of his comments, the angrier I became with him. It felt like we were both looking to argue and exploit each other's weakest points. That was not a liberating way for us to continue to engage. We can still be social justice advocates without speaking up every time we encounter a stereotype. Focus on the impact of what was said, not on the character flaws of the person who made the statement. As my mom used to say, "I don't dislike you, I dislike what you did."

### 2. **What are our common beliefs?**

Starting with where you agree can be a good way to build a relationship. Notice yourself listening for commonalities. At the same time, try to reframe your thinking from a "yes, but" approach to a "yes, and" approach. Simply switching this around, saying what you disagree with first and then where you see similarities, shifts the focus of the conversation to one of learning rather than debate. For example, "I define racism differently than you do. I see it as unintentional and institutional, not just individual bad actions. However, I can see we both view racism as problematic and something we want to change."

### 3. **Was there a point in my life when I saw the world like this person does?**

We learn about racism, power, and privilege through our experiences and education. Most of us, if honest with ourselves, can look back and recall a period of time in our life when we had less understanding. When engaging with someone who is inexperienced in these conversations, try to remember what it used to be like when you thought that way or imagine the world from their perspective. Asking questions that cause them to examine another perspective will usually work better than talking about facts or ideas from your broader knowledge of racism and privilege, especially if you are using unfamiliar language. Think about the Matryoshka dolls (Russian dolls that fit inside each other). The smaller doll inside can't see there is a larger doll around it, so that larger worldview seems meaningless.

### 4. What shapes this person's worldview?

Often, viewpoints that don't take privilege into account are built on a foundation of individual experiences and understandings, rather than that of the collective. An example of this is the "I was poor growing up and I made it" point of view. Asking questions that encourage the person to examine how they came to their conclusions can demonstrate their lack of foundation, acknowledging their personal experiences that may differ from that of the larger collective.

Asking questions forces the people you are conversing with to do most of the hard work. Sometimes, simply showing you understand their perspectives and then sharing your perspective encourages them to think more deeply. Active listening involves truly trying to see another point of view rather than planning your next argument. It is much more difficult to dismiss someone else's perspective when you care deeply about them and when you know they have taken the time to really understand where you're coming from.

# Chapter Twelve

## Common Examples of Triggering Events

**A** triggering event is not necessarily a bad thing to have happen in conversations about racism and privilege. In fact, these can be the moments of greatest learning. Because we want to take the conversation deeper, rather than avoid or attack, it is important to be able to identify what triggers us as facilitators. The exercises here and in chapter 13 are adapted from Kathy Obear, Alliance for Change.

Directions: Use a 0 to 5 scale to rate how much of a "trigger" each of the following is for you when facilitating a race relations workshop or discussion.

| No reaction 0 | Very mild 1 | Low 2 | Moderate 3 | Medium-high 4 | High 5 |
|---|---|---|---|---|---|

*Rate your emotional reaction.*

**As a facilitator when someone ...**

1. makes an offensive comment. ____
2. demonstrates racist attitudes and behaviors. ____
3. belittles my point or that of a participant. ____
4. calls a participant a racist. ____
5. criticizes my style or approach to communicating. ____
6. dominates the conversation and airtime. ____
7. interrupts me or others. ____
8. whines and clings to me or others. ____
9. demonstrates controlling behavior. ____
10. refuses to participate in the discussion or activity. ____
11. tries to "bully" me or others. ____
12. tells another participant how they should feel or behave. ____
13. is arrogant and self-righteous. ____
14. portrays themselves as the "victim" of "reverse discrimination." ____
15. jokes, has side conversations, or makes snide or sarcastic remarks. ____
16. questions my competency or point of view. ____
17. challenges mine or others' comments or behaviors as oppressive. ____

18. is experiencing and expressing deep emotions of pain or grief. ____
19. expresses anger. ____
20. makes oppressive comments about members of their own race. ____
21. refuses to own their privilege. ____
22. tries to derail the topic to some other -ism. ____
23. refuses to engage in any further dialogue. ____
24. is preoccupied with knitting, grading papers, or some other distraction. ____
25. says race conversations are unproductive (particularly a person of color). ____

## As a facilitator when ...
1. I make a mistake. ____
2. I do or say something oppressive. ____
3. I can't figure out how to manage a situation. ____
4. someone is angry with me. ____
5. there is intense conflict. ____
6. someone tries to correct me or criticizes me. ____
7. the conversation reactivates something from my past. ____

# Chapter Thirteen

## Restructure Self-Talk

If you're addicted to other people liking you, let it go. You can't please everyone.

—Keith Smith

**STOP your thoughts!**

When you've identified you're being triggered, the next step is to shift the way you're thinking about the person or the conversation. Refocus on what is happening in the moment.

1. **Positive Self-Talk**
   a. I can handle this.
   b. I've done this before.
   c. I am a competent, talented person.
   d. I have a lot to offer this person.
   e. I care.

## 2. **Calming Self-Talk**

    a. Breathe … steady …

    b. I don't have to know everything.

    c. I don't have to have the "perfect" answer.

    d. I'm doing the best I can. I don't have to be the expert.

    e. This isn't about me. Don't take this personally.

    f. How important is it to _____ ?

## 3. **Empathetic Self-Talk**

    a. I wonder what this person really needs, what they are really feeling?

    b. I wonder what they feel threatened or scared about?

    c. How can I better understand where this person is coming from?

    d. When have I felt similarly?

    e. I wonder what has been this person's experience that they respond this way?

## 4. **Recognize the Person's Level of Competence**

    a. They don't understand _____ .

    b. They don't have the ability to do what I want them to do at this time.

    c. They are doing the best they can with what they know.

    d. This work takes significant skill.

    e. It takes a long time to unlearn all this prejudice and socialization.

## 5. **Explore Your Part in the Situation**

    a. I wonder why I am so triggered.

    b. What else is going on for me?

    c. Which of my issues and needs are being triggered in this interaction?

    d. What needs of mine are not getting met?

    e. Who does this person remind me of?

    f. What personal issues are interfering with my willingness or ability to be helpful?

## 6. **Could I have triggered them …?**

    a. Am I contributing to their behavior?

    b. Have I acted inappropriately?

    c. What rules or expectations have I set up that are not working?

## 7. **Restructure Irrational Beliefs**

| Instead of | Try |
|---|---|
| I have to be liked and approved of by everyone. | Some people may not like me. In fact, if this is a useful interaction, people may leave feeling confused and full of unsettling emotions. |
| I must be competent in all situations and not make mistakes. | If I make a mistake, I can use it as an example in the conversation. They will see that I am human just like they are. |
| I have to know all the answers. | I do not have to be the expert on all things. My role here is to facilitate their coming to their own answers and finding their own voice. |
| I must remain calm and control my feelings. | If I get upset, I know I can manage my emotions. I could even use the event as a learning opportunity in the conversation. |
| I am responsible for their learning and growth. | I will do the best I can. I am not responsible for everyone's learning. People will take away from here what they need. |
| People who don't work to value difference are bad and should be blamed and punished. | They could be me not too long ago… I see myself in them. I want to help them learn from this experience. |
| I must try to change people to think and behave as I think they should. | I have no right to try to change people. I can share my experience, strength, and hope, and talk about the impact of their behavior on me and others. Who am I to know what they need? |

## 8. **Change Your Interpretation of the Event**

| If | Interpret |
|---|---|
| Someone is resistant: | They seem to feel safe enough to be honest about their thoughts and feelings. **OR** Now we can get to the heart of this issue. |
| Someone interrupts: | I don't appreciate their timing, but they have a legitimate point/question. **OR** They seem to have a lot of energy about this topic. |
| Someone makes a prejudicial remark: | Well, they came by their biases honestly in this society. **OR** I wonder what they fear? |
| Someone is angry: | I wonder what feelings of hurt or fear are under their anger? |
| Someone gives negative feedback: | I can model how to be open to feedback. **OR** This could be a powerful learning opportunity for me and others. **OR** Maybe I have something to learn here. |
| If I make a mistake or make a prejudicial remark: | I can model how to be nondefensive and honestly acknowledge my comment. **OR** I can model to own and apologize for the impact of my behavior. |

# Chapter Fourteen

## Assessing Your Triggers

The real art of conversation is not only to say the right thing at the right place but to leave unsaid the wrong thing at the tempting moment.

—Dorothy Neville

### 10 COMMON RESPONSES TO INTERCULTURAL TENSION AND CONFLICT

Triggers are those times when we may find our heart rate increase, our palms get sweaty, our voice cracks, our shoulders tense up, or any other number of physiological reactions. Being able to identify how you personally respond to triggers can help you consciously notice and shift your initial response. The better we understand ourselves, the more likely we are to be able to facilitate a difficult process for others.

Complete this table marking an "x" for how you generally respond when there is tension and/or strong emotion in a conversation.

| | Usually | Sometimes | Rarely | Never |
|---|---|---|---|---|
| Withdrawal, avoidance, isolation | | | | |
| Anxiety, nervousness, fear | | | | |
| Confusion, frustration | | | | |
| Ignoring it, going on as if nothing happened | | | | |
| Powerlessness, helplessness, apathy | | | | |
| Hostility, aggression, anger | | | | |
| Blaming, shaming, belittling, judging | | | | |
| Self-blame, feelings of inferiority/deviance | | | | |
| Joking, minimizing, making light of it | | | | |
| Engaging and embracing | | | | |

## STOP AND REFLECT

1. Write about a time when you responded in a way that shut down or stunted the conversation. What would you change?
2. Is this a typical response for you? Why do you think that is?

_____

_____

_____

_____

_____

_____

_____

_____

Adapted from Intercultural Laboratory, T547 class at CSPP-LA.

# Chapter Fifteen

## Racial Microaggressions

The greatest challenge society and the mental health profession face is making the "invisible" visible.

—Derald W. Sue, on racism

*Examine the impact, not the intent.*

Racial microaggressions are the subtle expressions of racism that are more commonly seen or heard today. They are often unintentionally hurtful words, phrases, or actions that trigger an emotional reaction from the person to whom the message is directed. Knowing the various themes of microaggressions will help you to be prepared to respond when they come up in a workshop. Two of the three types of microaggressions, microinsults and microinvalidations, happen frequently in everyday conversations but especially in conversations about race. As a facilitator it will be important that you address them rather than assume people are not bothered by them or that you can just move on because no one spoke up. Discussing the underlying message in what was said is a learning opportunity for all involved, and you'll need to encourage participants to recognize they can and do cause harm, even with the best of intentions.

### Microassault

- Conscious and purposeful
- Usually said in private; behind closed doors
- Racial epithets
- Discriminatory actions
- Displayed publicly when person loses control
- Discourages interracial interactions

**Microinsult**

- Subtle snubs
- Often unintentional
- Conveys a hidden insulting message
- Demeans racial heritage or identity
- Can occur nonverbally
- Context is important

**Microinvalidation**

- Negates reality of person of color
- Nullifies feelings, experiences
- Color blindness

*Source*: Sue et al. 2007.

# Chapter Sixteen

## Hot Buttons

Waiting five seconds allows everyone to at least think about what they want to say—or not say. Waiting five seconds allows learners to leave us believing they are brilliant and not that we are.

—Dr. Joye Norris

When someone commits a racial microaggression, they are usually unaware that they have offended. Microaggressions are subtle and usually intended as a compliment, and yet they have a hidden meaning usually imbedded in a stereotype. It's the underlying, hidden message that offends the listeners. Because the person means well, they are likely to take on a defensive posture when it is brought to their attention. Here are some examples of microaggressions, things said that push peoples hot buttons.

- Are you Chinese?
- Blacks and other minorities:

- Can I see two pieces of ID?
- Do you live in a tepee?
- Do you work here?
- I don't see color.
- I don't think of myself as white.
- We're victims too.
- I don't think of you as Mexican.
- I grew up poor, and I made it.
- I'm not prejudiced; my wife is Asian.
- I'm part Native American myself.
- It was just a joke.
- My best friend is black.
- The only race is the human race.
- I treat all people as equals.
- My ancestors didn't own slaves.
- Now that Obama's president, we can get beyond race.
- What happened to "the best man wins"?
- People need to speak English in the United States.
- Calm down.
- I hate all people equally.
- We need to transcend race.
- Those people . . .
- There's only one race, the human race.
- That's not what I meant.
- They're playing the race card.
- Sorry, I didn't see you.
- How long will whites have to pay for the sins of slavery?
- The most qualified person should get the job.
- Those people want something for nothing.
- We manifest our reality.
- Where are you really from?

## STOP AND REFLECT

List some of the trigger words or statements you have heard or used.

## THE WHO, WHAT, WHERE, WHEN, WHY, AND HOW APPROACH TO MICROAGGRESSIONS

It's easy to jump to the enemy image when someone offends. However, this approach rarely, if ever, works. Unfortunately, sometimes we can't help ourselves from becoming instantly angered. There are also those times when we start off calm, but the person is not open to hearing how their words offended, and as a result we get riled up. Try to see the other as human, and recognize they have been socialized to think and believe what they do. Their identity is at stake, and they feel they have a lot to lose when your focus is on their impact as opposed to their intent. So tread lightly, and in those moments do your best to become curious about them so they will learn and grow in the process.

- *What is the offender trying to convey?* If the person is trying to pay you a compliment, show you understand their intentions before telling them about the impact.
- *Who else thinks this way?* Microaggressions are such not because they occur once but because of all the times they are said. When someone commits a microaggression, it can feel like the straw that broke the camel's back. Share with the person that you have experienced this comment many times and why it hurts or why it does not feel like a compliment.
- *Why is the offender defensive?* The person who offended has likely worked very hard at being sensitive to race issues and probably prides themselves on this fact. If there is anything you can share with them that shows you see this in them, tell them.
- *Where is a good entry point to engage them?* It's difficult to know when to point out the offense, but timing is important. Because microaggressions happen as a part of everyday conversation, they often occur in the middle of a personal story, or even when simply asking a question or commenting on something. In any of these cases, pointing out a microaggression takes away from what they are trying to say and shifts the conversation to the offending remark. Try to be sensitive to timing. It can make a difference as to whether they will hear you or not.
- *When have they had experiences that would cause them to think any differently?* For many, the answer is "rarely, if ever." Many people were taught at an early age to operate from color-blind ideology and as a result say and do things that are offensive without meaning to offend. People who have less experience and exposure to diversity rely more heavily on words that have been deemed in the past as safe as a way to convey they are not like "those people who are clearly racist." If you can remember it took time for you to get to the place you're currently at, it might help you to be sensitive to where they're at. Remind others of this fact.
- *How do I engage them?* This is the question of the century. As we have mentioned many times, the "how" comes with practice, and even then you will find yourself in situations where you thought you figured out the "how" only to find that this time and in this situation on this particular day, your "how" was ineffective. We are not trying to make you feel like this work is impossible to facilitate, we just don't want to oversimplify our strategies. Below are some suggestions on how you can engage a participant when they have committed a microaggression.

### 1. **Pause the Conversation**

Let the group know you're shifting from the agenda or current topic to talk about something happening in the room.

   a. *Let's pause this dialogue for a moment to talk about what just happened.*
   b. *Leonard (POC), rather than answer Sharon's question about whether race was really factor in your experience, I would like a moment to pause here and, instead, discuss the question being asked.*

### 2. **Acknowledge Comments as Microaggressions**

While the term *microaggression* has been around since the early 1970s, when Chester Pierce first coined the term, it is relatively new language that gained nationwide attention when Sue and colleagues (2007) first published an article on the subject. As a result, people are finding new language to describe their everyday experiences. Conversations are shifting from, "There's something about what that person said that bothered me, but I'm not quite sure what it is," to, for example, "I felt troubled by your statement 'You're not like the others.' I know you meant it as a compliment, but it's a microaggression that I experience often. It reminds me of how often people stereotype people who look like me, and when they don't fit that stereotype, they are seen as the exception to the rule rather than an example of our diversity." This type of response is helpful to everyone involved. It opens up dialogue. Being able to name exactly what was offensive, and why, is also empowering. The person who offended has the opportunity to gain understanding. As a facilitator, practice engaging people in everyday situations when you witness, commit, or experience a microaggression. It will help prepare you for facilitating in a large group setting. The following are some suggestions for introducing microaggressions into the conversation when someone has offended:

a. *Has anyone seen the recent research that came out by Derald Sue? He co-authored a few articles and published two books on the topic, including microaggressions for gender, race, and sexual orientations. His research helps us to understand subtle unconscious and unintentional statements that we all often make with positive intent but that actually have a negative impact on the recipient.*

b. *Heidi, I've heard that comment made before, and usually it is said with positive intent. What most people don't realize is the subtle hidden message in that type of statement. For example, when someone says to an African-American person that they sound articulate, it reinforces the stereotype that blacks are not intelligent. When you said to Kim that you don't think of her as Asian, do you have any thoughts about the underlying message it conveys, even though it was meant as a compliment?*

Heidi is not likely to know what the hidden message is, otherwise she wouldn't have said it. In this case, you would want to open up the question to the whole group. To help prevent thinking that only Heidi commits microaggressions, have a few participants share other types of microaggressions they have heard or spoken.

c. *This is a great learning opportunity for all of us. A common experience people of color have is someone questioning whether race was really involved in the situation. This is referred to as a microinvalidation. What might be the impact on our relationships across cultures when people of color receive those types of comments in response to their naming experiences of racism?*

This type of statement tries to get participants to understand why it's important they remain open to understanding. Many believe having conversations about race divides us. In actuality, it's usually their defensiveness and unwillingness to be open to exploring racism that shuts the conversation down and causes a rift between us.

### 3. Comment on the Reaction That Occurred in the Room

Doing this work requires that we take risks and actually name what was said, speak directly to whoever said it, normalize their having made the comment, and then talk about how we experienced it. While it might feel more comfortable to you to skirt around what happened by talking about it in a general way, everyone in the room will know whom you are talking about. This is a time to become comfortable with the discomfort and model having courageous conversations. You will become more comfortable with practice.

a. *I noticed that a lot of people reacted when Liz said, "those people." Would anyone be willing to share what their reactions were so Liz and others in the room have some understanding of what that comment brings up in people?*

b. *This is a great opportunity to practice our norm of experiencing discomfort. Did anyone notice a shift in the room when Aaron said, "Orientals"?*

c. *We haven't talked about microaggressions today. Has anyone heard of that term?* (Wait for response.) *What can you share about it?* (Wait for answer.). *Thank you.* (Define it.) *I asked because I noticed that there was a reaction in the room to something Julie just said. My guess is that she had no idea that what she said may have offended some people. Since we are here to talk and learn about race relations, this would be a good time to use this as an opportunity to teach everyone in the room about microaggressions. While I don't have time to go into too much detail, sometimes just acknowledging it in our conversation can be helpful so that it doesn't stand between us.* (During or after the conversation connect with Julie so that she doesn't feel like the bad target.)

### 4. Setting the Stage to Decrease Defensiveness

While some people disagree with our style of minimizing blame, shame, and guilt, we have tried the "hit 'em hard" strategy and found it just doesn't work in the majority of situations. This approach feels like an attack to the recipient, and as a result they will usually become defensive and attack back to protect their integrity. Consequently, when we facilitate we are constantly trying to think of ways to engage the offender to reduce defensiveness and to avoid belittling and blaming the person on the receiving end. We find this approach increases the probability the offender will be more open to listening and the offended more likely to be heard. Below are examples for setting the stage for the conversation to increase the likelihood they will be open to hearing the impact of their words.

a. *Before we engage Tammy concerning what she said, I want to first point out we have all been guilty at one time or another of saying or doing something that offended another person and triggered an emotional reaction in them. In these moments, we are unconsciously incompetent and don't know what we don't know. The real challenge is finding ways to stay present enough to engage in conversations about how what was said made the other person feel so that we can learn from the experience. As we engage in conversation around what Tammy said, it's helpful in our learning if we practice strategies that don't shame, blame, or guilt one another into understanding. This will help take us to conscious competence and eventually unconscious competence.*

b. *Once someone says something that triggers an emotional response in us it can be very difficult to stay present in the conversation. Let's take a moment to talk about what was said that triggered your reaction and how it made you feel, and then check in with Liz* (who triggered the response), *giving her the opportunity to deepen her understanding and convey to us what she intended.*

### 5. Remind Participants That We Are Here to Learn from One Another

Before engaging in conversations about the microaggression that was committed, remind participants of the purpose and objectives for the workshop.

a. *I realize what was just said probably pushed some hot buttons in the room, but before we engage in courageous conversation around it, I want to remind people one of the core reasons for each of us being here is to learn and grow in our understanding of race issues. The best way to make this happen is to share our thoughts in a way that honors and values the humanity of everyone in this space. It's also important to remember that in order to learn we have to be open to hearing another person's perspective.*

b. *Bryce, you made a comment that triggered some reactions, and there are likely other people in the room who see things the same way that you do. I had planned to have us unpack a vignette later in the day, but your statement gives us the opportunity to learn from one another using a real situation. It will be challenging for all of us, but if everyone is willing, let's see if we can navigate our way through courageous conversations in the here and now.*

c. *When someone shares how they were affected by the microaggression, they are essentially offering a gift to the person who has offended. The gift comes in the form of an opportunity for the other to gain understanding. At the same time, that person is taking a risk that their experience will be dismissed or minimized. What happens more often than not in these situations is when we share with someone that their words have offended us, they become defensive, usually in the form of "that's not what I meant," or "it was just a joke," or "you are taking it too seriously." This signals to the person offended that the person is not open to hearing, and the impact goes unexplored. It is not uncommon for that person to keep the rest of their thoughts to themselves and talk with someone who understands. These are examples of what makes an environment feel unwelcoming and divides us in our intercultural relationships. In the spirit of wanting to create a more inclusive environment for all people, and to learn from experience, I'm hoping, Kim, you'll try to listen for understanding and accept the gift Charles is offering to you, even though it will be difficult, because your intentions were good.*

## 6. **Tie the Conversation or Experience to the Norms**

Reminding participants of the norms before diving into courageous conversations is an effective way to make the transition. It reminds them of what to expect and normalizes the difficulty of the conversation. We tend to name 1 to 3 norms that we think will particularly apply to the situation.

a. *Okay, I see people reacting to what was just said, but before we engage in courageous conversations I want to remind everyone of the norms, particularly, "experience discomfort and listen for understanding."*

b. *Ariana, you just said, "We can never really understand someone else's reality." I'm wondering if you would restate that as your truth by saying, "I can ..."* (She does.) *How did that feel different?*

c. *I've noticed we haven't heard from some of you, and I'm guessing not everyone in the room agrees or is on the same page. This is a good time to take risks. Remember, if not here, where can we have these conversations?*

## 7. **Allow Participants to Tell Their Stories**

Providing people the opportunity to share their story helps to lessen the "enemy image" by acknowledging that we are shaped and socialized to think the way we do.

*Susan, I don't know if you realize it or not, but I'm sensing what you just said triggered an emotional reaction from some people in the room. I think it would make sense if we stopped here for a moment and had some conversation about this before moving on. This may be a learning opportunity for all of us.* (Ask a few participants in the room to share their reactions to what Susan said, but not so many that she feels overwhelmed and shuts down). After a few participants have shared ask, *Susan, what are you hearing from your colleagues? Would you be willing to share with us how you came to understand or see things the way you do that led you to that comment? It could be something you were taught or experienced growing up.*

## 8. Expect and Accept Nonclosure

Remember, Glenn Singleton's norms are not just for the participants to keep in mind. They will also serve you well in your role as facilitator. "Accept and Expect Nonclosure" is a norm that you will find yourself having to practice more times than you would prefer because if you let it, courageous conversations could continue on for hours. As the facilitator, you will need to decide when it is time to move on. Next are examples to help you gauge the situation.

Don't determine if the conversation should continue based on whether learning has occurred for the person who has offended. While growth is what you hope for, it may be the person is not ready.

Don't allow one person's learning to take up too much of the whole group's time. If some-one seems resistant to learning from their mistakes but the majority of the group demonstrates understanding, you can continue with the planned agenda. Remind participants in that moment to expect and accept on nonclosure.

Sometimes many participants will be affected and want to comment on the microaggres-sion that was committed. This is often done through the sharing of stories by both whites and participants of color. While this conveys comradeship and is often intended to "convince" the offender to "see the light," when too many participants are allowed to share, it usually results in the offender feeling ganged up on. You will have to pay close attention to the feeling in the room and determine when enough sharing has happened. One strategy is to encourage partici-pants to continue to engage one another during lunch.

*I can tell by the number of hands that went up that Mary's comment affected a lot of people. I'm concerned that we have already spent quite a bit of time on this. We have probably learned everything we're going to at this time in this way. However, I encourage you to continue the conversation with each other beyond this workshop. Mary, I'm hoping you will continue to reflect and process this experience. I hope we all will.*

If you take the risk out of life, you take the opportunity out of life.

—Keith Smith

## Ordering Hot Buttons:

To order a bag of hot buttons to lead participants in an activity to increase their understanding of racial microaggressions, visit our website at http://culturesconnecting.com/products/.

## STOP AND REFLECT

1. Recall a time when you witnessed, committed, or experienced a racial microaggression.
2. Did you respond? If not, why not? If so, how did you respond?
3. What would you do differently if given another chance with the same situation?

_____

_____

_____

_____

_____

_____

_____

_____

_____

_____

_____

_____

_____

_____

# Chapter Seventeen

## Racial Microaggression Themes

When we come at people with our own painful emotions it's often very hard for them to hear the legitimacy of our concerns. When we listen to them, it is much easier for them to hear our concerns in return.

—Cherrie Brown and George Mazza

Sue and colleagues organized racial microaggressions into themes. Following are examples of themes from a school setting. As you read through, them think about how these themes materialize where you live and work.

| Theme | Microaggression | Message |
|-------|-----------------|---------|
| **Alien in One's Own Country:** When Asian Americans and Latin@s are assumed to be foreign born. | Asking an Asian co-worker, "Where are you from? No, where are you *really* from?" Telling an American-born Latin@ they speak such good English. | You are not American. |
| **Ascription of Intelligence:** Assigning a degree of intelligence to a person of color on the basis of their race. | A school counselor reacting with surprise when an Asian-American student had trouble on the math test. | All Asians are smart and good at math. |
| | A career counselor asking a black or Latin@ student, "Do you think you're ready for college?" | It is unusual for people of color to succeed academically. |

| **Color Blindness:** Statements which indicate that a person does not want to acknowledge race. | A staff member of color attempts to discuss what it's like being one of few people of color in the workplace and feeling dismissed and marginalized. A white staff member says, "Don't you think you're being a little too sensitive? We should focus on similarities not people's differences." When a student complains that a teacher is racist, and another teacher replies, "We don't see color here on our campus. We just see individuals." | Race and culture are not important variables that affect people's lives. <br><br><br><br> Your racial experiences are not valid. |
|---|---|---|
| **Criminality/Assumption of Criminal Status:** A person of color is presumed to be dangerous, criminal, or deviant on the basis of their race. | At night, black students are consistently stopped and questioned on campus but their white peers are not. | You are a criminal. |
| **Denial of Individual Racism:** A statement made when whites renounce their racial biases. | A new hire asks her supervisor if race is addressed in the organization. The supervisor replies, "Race does not affect the way we work with one another. We treat everyone the same." A student of color brings up racism with a female teacher. She replies, "I totally understand. As a woman, I face discrimination, too." | Your racial/ethnic experience is not important. <br><br><br><br> Your racial oppression is no different from my gender oppression. |
| **Myth of Meritocracy:** Statements which assert that race does not play a role in succeeding in career advancement or education. | A co-worker says to a colleague, "This is America. Anyone can succeed if they work hard enough." When a staff member of color complains about being passed over for promotion, his colleague replies, "Maybe if you work harder you'll get promoted next time." | People of color are lazy and/or incompetent and need to work harder. <br><br> If you don't succeed, you have only yourself to blame (blaming the victim). |
| **Pathologizing Cultural Values/ Communication Styles:** The notion that the values and communication styles of the dominant/white culture are the norm. | A Black man speaks loudly with affect when engaging in discussion with co-workers. One of the co-workers complains to her supervisor and says she is fearful and sees his behavior as inappropriate. An Asian or Native American employee doesn't maintain eye contact with her supervisor. The supervisor assumes she is being disrespectful. | Assimilate to dominant culture. <br><br><br><br> Leave your cultural baggage outside. Not maintaining eye contact is unacceptable. |

| | | |
|---|---|---|
| **Second-Class Citizen:** Occurs when a white person is given preferential treatment as a consumer over a person of color. | White staff members get called on more often and are more frequently asked their opinions in staff meetings. A white student is served first by the office staff but a student of color arrived first. | Whites are more valued than people of color.<br><br>White students are more valued than students of color. |
| **Environmental Microaggressions:** Macro-level microaggressions, which are more apparent on a systemic level. | The magazines in the lobby and pictures on the wall are geared toward the white dominant culture. White people are the protagonists of all of the required reading in class. | You don't belong; only white people can succeed.<br><br>You are an outsider; you don't exist. |

Adapted from Sue et al. 2007.

# Chapter Eighteen

## Crossroads to Reinforcing Cycles in Relationships

We are caught in an inescapable network of mutuality, tied in a single garment of destiny. Whatever affects one directly, affects all indirectly.

—Martin Luther King Jr.

When we come to a crossroads in our conversation, we make a choice about the path we will follow. Often, our response triggers a similar response in the other person, and we end up in a cycle of attacking, avoiding, or engaging. By consciously thinking about what we want the outcome of the conversation to be, we can choose a path that will more likely bring people into the conversation. Daniel B. Wile, in his book *Collaborative Couples Therapy: Turning Fights into Intimate Conversations*, gives three of the most common types of responses to conflict. The chart below was adapted and gives examples of each.

| Crossroads | Reinforcing Cycle | Outcome |
|---|---|---|
| ATTACK—react or defend: You express what you are feeling or how you are experiencing what was just said in the form of a complaint or attack by criticizing or retaliating. Hot buttons are usually pushed. | Turns the other person into an enemy and often triggers an adversarial cycle. Each person has a comeback that one-ups the other person or shuts the other down when stung too badly by their words. Neither person feels heard by the other. | Turns each other into ENEMIES |
| AVOID—withdraw or downplay: You keep your thoughts to yourself, change the subject, or minimize what is said to avoid having a courageous conversation. The conversation is over. | Turns the other person into a stranger who never really gets to know you or how you experience the world. Often triggers a withdrawn cycle. Each person avoids saying what they really feel. | Turns each other into STRANGERS |

| ENGAGE—confide, listen, and ask questions with genuine curiosity: You bring the person in for an honest conversation about how you are experiencing what they have said. You also take in and believe what they are trying to tell you. Ask questions that probe deeper into their experiences. | Turns the other person into an ally, triggering an empathic collaborative cycle. | Turns each other into ALLIES |
|---|---|---|

## Example

| Allison's Comment<br>White Woman | Janet's Response<br>African-American Woman | |
|---|---|---|
| ATTACK:<br>Why does the conversation always have to center around race? I was poor growing up, and I made it. I'm tired of hearing excuses for why someone isn't successful. If you work hard you can succeed! | **Attack:** Yeah, well that's easy for you to say coming from a place of white privilege! People don't necessarily know that you were poor. They don't treat you like you're inferior the moment they see you!<br>**Avoid:** Eyes rolling, sidebar conversation—can you believe what she just said—or saves thoughts for a person of color.<br>**Engage:** Yes, I worry about that too. Poverty is a serious issue. It sounds like you are feeling frustrated that your experiences are left out of the conversation and don't count. I certainly don't want this conversation to become the oppression Olympics, one where we try to one-up each other and no one gets heard. I don't know if you intended this, but when you said you're tired of people making excuses, I felt myself become angry and defensive. Maybe we could hear each other better and understand one another's experiences by starting with some of the institutional barriers you faced growing up poor, and then I will share mine. | |

| | | |
|---|---|---|
| AVOID:<br>I treat all people the same regardless of their race. Talking about racial differences just divides us. We should talk about our similarities, not our differences. | **Attack:** First of all, the fact that you treat everyone the same (if that's even possible) is part of the problem! Second of all, you may think talking about race divides us, but it's actually not talking about race that divides us. That's just like white people to try and skirt around the issue of race and talk about something else so that they don't have to take responsibility for their white privilege!<br>**Avoid:** All of the issues—sexual orientation, ability, gender, class, race, etc.—are important. It's hard to know what to talk about. (Changes subject) What was the name of that restaurant you said you liked?<br>**Engage:** Recognizing that we have more in common than not is important. Can you say a little more about your concern that having conversations about our differences will divide us? It sounds like you're worried it will affect our relationship. I'd like to try to understand where you are coming from and how you see things. | |
| ENGAGE:<br>I'm embarrassed and a little afraid to say this because I'm not sure how people will respond, but I've always struggled with understanding how race matters. I guess it's hard for me as a white woman who grew up poor to understand how a person's race holds them back. I don't feel like being white has been an advantage. I need you to help me understand where you are coming from with this. | **Attack:** A person's race doesn't hold them back, it's the views others have of them because of their race and the way they are treated that holds them back!<br>**Avoid:** Well, don't worry; it's difficult for a lot of people to understand.<br>**Engage:** This is a difficult issue that requires intentionality to understand and I appreciate your willingness. I know for me I've had to attend a lot of workshops, read, and then engage in a lot of conversations to be able to see beyond my own experiences. I feel heard when you are willing to take risks and engage in courageous conversations. Tell me more about your experience growing up so I can better understand where you are coming from in all this. | |

Adapted from Wile 2009.

## STOP AND REFLECT

1. In what types of situations do you tend to attack, avoid, or engage when in conflict? (E.g., you might avoid expressing your thoughts with authority but attack with your spouse or partner.)
2. Think of a situation where you were in conflict and were able to engage. What did you do well?
3. Think of a situation where you were in conflict and you avoided or attacked. What could you have said or done differently to engage effectively?

_____

_____

_____

_____

_____

_____

_____

_____

_____

_____

_____

_____

_____

# Chapter Nineteen

## Learning Conversation Stems

The only reason we don't open our hearts and minds to other people is that they trigger confusion in us that we don't feel brave enough or sane enough to deal with. To the degree that we look clearly and compassionately at ourselves, we feel confident and fearless about looking into someone else's eyes.

—Pema Chödrön

The following phrases and questions can help you to effectively engage in courageous conversations. Make them your own and think about what you might add to this list. Practice is key to success!

### THE PERSON WHO OFFENDED

*In order for this to work, it's important you be open to understanding how your words or actions affected the other person and you ...*
  - *try to connect with the other person's feelings and needs.*
  - *show you are sincerely interested in them. (This is not just a technique.)*
  - *focus on contributing to their well-being. Meet them where they're at.*
  - *focus on impact instead of intent.*
  - *empathize, don't sympathize.*
  - *remember that their reality/experiences may differ from yours.*
  - *stay with it but don't force closure.*

*Engagement strategies for the person who offended:*

1. What impact have my actions had on you?
2. It seems like you might be having an emotional reaction to what I just said, and I'm wondering if you would be willing to engage me in conversation around it.
3. How did what I just said impact you? I notice you seem upset.
4. Can you say a little more about why you're so frustrated with me?

5. Were you reacting to something I did or said?
6. What was it that I said that caused your reaction?
7. Will you let me/us in on your thoughts?
8. I'm trying to understand these issues better; can you say more about _____.
9. I'm trying my best to grasp what you're saying, but it's difficult for me given how new I am to these conversations. Could you give another example of what you mean by _____?
10. I'm nervous having this conversation because I worry what you will think of me, but I will do my best to stay in it. Are you saying that _____?
11. Let me see if I'm hearing you right; you're saying that _____.
12. I'm truly sorry for having offended you. I had no idea that my words had those subtle implications. Have I ever said anything like that before that has offended you?
13. I'm trying to listen for understanding, but I'm struggling to fully understand how _____? Would you say more about that?
14. May I start over?
15. Thank you for taking the risk to share how my words affected you. Is there something else I should be aware of?
16. I'm hearing that when I said _____, I revealed an unconscious stereotype about _____. Thank you for taking the risk to share that with me. I didn't know the impact of my words. I'm sorry.

## THE PERSON WHO WAS OFFENDED

---

*If you are the target of a microaggression, and you at first attacked or avoided the conversation and now want to engage, it's important that you ...*
- *work not to keep the enemy image. See what's good in them.*
- *don't insult or educate.*
- *try to connect with the other person.*
- *think about what are the needs of the other person? Why did they say or do what they did?*
- *don't punish, shame, blame, or guilt them into understanding.*
- *meet them where they are at.*
- *move beyond a place of rightness and wrongness.*
- *give them grace to make mistakes.*

---

*Engagement strategies for the person who was offended:*

1. Would you be open to hearing how I experienced what you said?
2. Would you be open to hearing how I heard it?
3. Wait, can we pause the conversation and talk about what was just said?
4. I would like to tell you how your words affected me, but I'm worried you'll become defensive. When you said _____, I felt _____.
5. I'm having an emotional reaction to what you just said, and I'm wondering if you would be willing to engage in conversation about it.
6. What would it mean to you if that (racism, power, privilege, oppression) is still happening?
7. What are some of your thoughts about what is going on with _____? (Describe something having to do with racism, power, privilege.)
8. It would help me understand if you could share an example of _____.
9. Help me to better understand why you feel that way. Can you be more specific about how you came to believe _____?
10. I want to better understand your perspective. Would you give me an example of when your whiteness (for example) worked against you?
11. I'm hearing that your intent was _____. I can appreciate your good intentions, and I'm also wondering if you would be open to hearing what I heard when you said, "_____."

**Note:** When engaging, acknowledge what the person has said in a way that shows you understand. Ask questions that help the person think about how their experiences have influenced the way they see the world. It is also important to keep these norms in the center of the conversation. Listen for understanding, expect and accept nonclosure, speak your truth, stay engaged, experience discomfort, take risks, and don't engage in fixing.

## BOTH THE OFFENDED AND THE OFFENDER

> *It's important that we all ...*
> - *become good at asking questions.*
> - *give one another a chance to learn from our mistakes.*
> - *know that the other person's perspective is their reality.*
> - *avoid the posture that suggests all of our perspectives are 100% right.*
> - *are open to learning.*
> - *talk about our emotions in a way that helps the other understand them.*
> - *realize we all have prejudice and bias.*
> - *practice becoming skilled at communicating effectively.*

*Engagement strategies for the person who offended and the person who was offended:*

1. Shift from, "I understand," to "Can you help me understand ____?"
2. Tell me more about ____.
3. Can you say a little more about how you see things?
4. What information might you have that I don't?
5. How do you see it differently?
6. How are you feeling about all of this?
7. Say more about why this is important to you?
8. I'm wondering if it's possible to ____.
9. I'm wondering if it would make sense to ____.
10. I need you to help me understand where you are coming from on this.
11. I'm wondering whether we could talk about how we each reacted to that conversation and whether there's a better way we could address these issues.
12. What do you mean when you say ____?
13. I think I heard you say ____. (Paraphrase.) Did I understand that correctly?
14. I'm feeling (anxious, concerned, etc.) about having this conversation and how we're going to work together in the future. I'm also hopeful that we can trust each other enough to have difficult conversations. How are you feeling?
15. I know there are power dynamics in our relationship. How do you think that is influencing our conversation?
16. I'm wondering whether we could talk about how we each reacted to the conversation and whether there's a better way we could address the issue?
17. I'm hoping we can have a courageous conversation about what happened earlier because ____. (Name what's important about your relationship with that person.)
18. What's going on for you right now?
19. I noticed (name the nonverbal you observed) when I said, "____," you ____. What was that about? Would you be willing to talk about what was going on for you?

## SELF-HELP TOOLS

The Public Conversations Project developed the following participant self-help tool. You can provide this for participants at the start of the workshop or use it to guide your participants in dialogue.

- If you feel cut off, say so, or override the interruption.
  *I'd like to finish ...*
- If you feel misunderstood, clarify what you mean.
  *Let me put this another way...*
- If you feel misheard, ask the listener to repeat what they heard you say, then affirm or correct their statement.
- If you feel hurt or disrespected, say so. If possible, describe exactly what you heard or saw that evoked hurt feelings in you.
  *When you said ____, I felt ____.*
- If you feel angry, express the anger directly rather than expressing it or acting it out indirectly, for example, by trashing another person's statement or asking a sarcastic or rhetorical question.
  *I felt angry when I heard you say ____.*
- If you feel confused, frame a question that seeks clarification or more information. You may prefer to paraphrase what you have heard.
  *Are you saying ____?*
- If you feel uncomfortable with the process, state your discomfort and check in with the group to see how others are experiencing what is happening. If others share your concerns, and you have an idea about what would help, offer that idea.
  *I'm not comfortable with the tone this conversation has taken. How are others feeling? Can we take a minute to reconnect with why we all came here today?*
- If you feel the conversation is going off track, share your perception and check in with others.

## PATHWAYS TO A CONNECTED CONVERSATION

Successfully engaging in courageous conversations requires that we give a lot of ourselves. It is a vulnerable partnership that needs to be open and authentic between us. What's most challenging is you may be willing to be open, but the other person remains distant. You are only responsible for your part. You can't make anyone do anything they are not willing to do. However, if you give of yourself, it does become an invitation for others to do the same.

**Explore where each story comes from**
    "My reactions here probably have a lot to do with my previous experiences."
    "I've had some really bad experiences before while trying to have these conversations, and so it's difficult for me to ____."

**Share the impact on you**

"I don't know whether you intended this, but I felt extremely uncomfortable when _____."

"I know you didn't mean it this way, but when you said, _____, it made me think/feel _____."

**Take responsibility for your contribution**

"There are a number of things I've done that have made this situation harder."

"I'm not sure how, but I feel like I may have disrespected you in some way. I feel the tension between us; can we talk about it? I'm trying to become more consciously competent."

**Describe feelings**

"I'm anxious about bringing this up, but it's important to me that we talk about it."

"I'm not sure why, but I'm feeling uncomfortable right now with what was just said. Can we stop for a minute and talk about it?"

"When you said, _____. I instantly felt angry because it sounded like you were saying _____."

**Reflect on the identity issues**

"I think the reason this subject hooks me is that I don't like thinking of myself as someone who _____."

"It's hard for me to hear that what I'm saying is racist. I have always thought of myself as _____."

**Name the elephant in the room**

"I'm wondering how you feel about having a white (therapist, teacher, etc.) explore this issue with you. I imagine that if I was in your shoes I would be concerned about whether someone like me would understand your experiences."

**Build a Platform**

1. When you call someone's unconscious bias to their attention, they are likely to get defensive, which is often rooted in deep identity issues. Tell them how you see them as (e.g., caring, thoughtful, kind, open to learning, etc.), so you are not saying they are a bad person as a result of them offending you.
2. Tell them why you decided to talk with them (e.g., concern for your child, you value your relationship, you don't want to build resentment, your understanding of the impact on children).
3. Share a time when you have done something similar so they see you are not blaming them but see yourself as a learner, too.
4. Describe what they did or said, without judgment.
5. Circle back at the end of the conversation and share how you are feeling. "This was tough for me to bring this up with you, but I'm glad we talked about it. I don't want to start off on a bad note." Ask where they are at with this conversation: "How are you feeling?"

> I'm for truth, no matter who tells it. I'm for justice, no matter who it is for or against. I'm a human being, first and foremost, and as such I'm for whoever and whatever benefits humanity as a whole.
>
> —Malcolm X

Adapted from Stone et al. 1999.

## PRACTICE SCENARIOS

Read through Scenario 1 and discuss the questions. Scenario 2 provides you with the opportunity to review a past situation you experienced and think through what you would do differently.

### Scenario 1

When facilitating a group, Leticia, a Latina woman, begins crying while sharing her story of her upbringing. Though she grew up in a loving family, her family's experiences of racism living in a predominately white community and going to schools where she was the minority bring up painful memories.

Michelle, a white woman in the group, responds by saying, "I had a very difficult experience growing up, too. We were poor and struggled a great deal. Going to college was a huge challenge for me because I am the first in my family to ever receive a higher education. But I choose to focus on the positives in my life. When people focus on the negatives it keeps them in a victim mentality."

### QUESTIONS TO EXPLORE

1. What do you think is Michelle's intent in her response?
2. Identify the potential triggers and microaggressions in Michelle's response.
3. What messages might Leticia hear in Michelle's response?
4. How might Leticia be feeling?
5. Do you think Leticia is likely to attack, avoid, or engage you in this situation?
6. Imagine that you are Michelle and that you realize you have offended Leticia, but you don't know why or how. You have just taken a workshop on cross-cultural communication skills in which you learned about racial microaggressions and strategies for effectively engaging. You see this as an opportunity to practice engaging rather than avoiding the conversation.
   a. Using the Learning Conversation Stems, Pathways to a Connected Conversation, and your own best thinking, what could you say to engage Leticia on how you may have offended her? Highlight possible engagement strategies, and think of your own.
   b. Now try to place them in order of when you would say what.
   c. Don't oversimplify this. If you have offended Leticia, she is unlikely to open up right away or even at all—just because you said a few things to try to and engage her.

### Scenario 2

Each person in your group takes 3 minutes to share a time when they witnessed, committed, or experienced a microaggression, and how they responded.

1. Decide which one of the examples you would like to discuss more fully.
2. Discuss "Questions to Explore" below.

3. Once you have some ideas about what might be going on for those involved, talk about how you might respond differently if given the opportunity to do it over again. Use the Learning Conversation Stems, Pathways to a Connected Conversation, and your own best thinking.
4. Now try to place them in order of when you would say what.
5. If you have time, role-play the situation.
6. Decide who will role-play and who will observe. Debrief what went well and what was challenging.

## QUESTIONS TO EXPLORE

1. What was the intent and impact?
2. What were the possible triggers and microaggressions?
3. How might people be experiencing the situation from different perspectives?
4. What do you imagine everyone involved was feeling?
5. Did people "attack, avoid, or engage"?
6. Based on what you've learned so far, how might you approach the situation differently?

When the going gets tough, turn to wonder. Wonder what's going on with me, wonder what's going on with you.

—Unknown author

# SECTION IV

# COUNTERACTING EXPRESSIONS OF WHITE PRIVILEGE

We have observed some very important changes through which they [whites] seem to move as they work toward multicultural cultural competence (Sue 2011). We have been impressed with how Whites seem to go through parallel racial/cultural identity transformation. This is especially true if we accept the fact that Whites are as much victims of societal forces (i.e., they are socialized into racist attitudes and beliefs) as are their minority counterparts (D. W. Sue 2003). No child is born wanting to be a racist! Yet White people do benefit from the dominant–subordinate relationship in our society. It is this factor that Whites need to confront in an open and honest manner.

—Sue and Sue (2013, 331)

# Chapter Twenty

## Counteracting Expressions of White Privilege

White privilege is a system of unearned benefits afforded to those people classified as white. These advantages are personal, cultural, and institutional and provide greater access to resources and systemic power. For white people, white privilege leads to a form of internalized oppression because it distorts their relationships and humanity.

When facilitating dialogue about the social dynamics of oppression and privilege, it's important you remain aware that those dynamics are always present in the room. The ability to recognize and name privilege during a conversation about privilege requires knowledge, persistence, and practice. This includes noticing your own socialization to privilege whiteness and noticing the behaviors of participants.

Skilled facilitators not only recognize expressions of white privilege and counteract them, but they also use these instances as an opportunity to grow understanding. The following section spotlights several ways we've seen white privilege  manifested in workshops and classrooms. The responses are not designed to be memorized but, rather, to serve as a guide.

Many of the expressions of privilege we highlight are common across multiple forms of oppression. For example, members of dominant groups (heterosexual, male, wealthy, etc.) frequently reframe and reinterpret the experiences of members of marginalized groups to fit dominant paradigms. Dominating the conversation is a common form of male privilege—and white privilege. It is something that can occur automatically and unconsciously. As you read this section, think about how white privilege intersects with other types of privilege in participants' identities.

It is important to note that aspects of white supremacy culture have been internalized by both white people and people of color. Therefore, you may see some of the behaviors below perpetuated by people of color and by whites. For example, people of color may have learned to give more time and listen more attentively to white people's comments, may invalidate each other's experiences, and may participate in either/or thinking, among others. Your role is to help all participants in the discussion dig deep into the root of their behaviors and recognize our collective socialization. This will help us more effectively collaborate to eliminate white privilege.

### 1. Dominating the Conversation

Dominating the conversation can occur from any person, regardless of their race. It tends to happen when people are eager to process out loud what they've learned and share with others. It can also be a result of group cultural norms. For example, research shows that African Americans tend to talk fast, interrupt, and use their hands when speaking. They are less likely to adhere to the "take turns" norms that are often the protocol in group settings. While this learned style of communication is not evident in all African Americans, it is a common, unspoken social norm that those who want to speak need to jump in if they want to be heard. This differs from whites, who are unconsciously socialized to believe their opinions and voices are more valuable than those of people of color. There are strategies for interrupting any participants discussed earlier in this book, but this section focuses specifically on white privilege.

When white people dominate the conversation, it contributes to sustaining white culture's norm of individualism. Rather than collaboratively sharing airtime and learning from one another, dominating the conversation reinforces hierarchies that don't allow for full participation of some members of the group. White people may feel pressure to speak up, falsely believing they have to take on a leadership role in small or large groups.

Dominating the conversation can also take the form of asking the most questions in group discussions. If the majority of the time is spent addressing one person's question, that person is still dominating the conversation, even if they aren't speaking. While asking questions and processing is important to learning new information, whites need to be mindful of the impact this has on others in the room, and of the coupling of being heard more than others with internalized superiority.

### FACILITATOR'S ROLE

Notice whom you invite to share their thoughts, either through body language, such as eye contact, or verbal interaction. Actively counter your own internalization of whose voices are more important. Interrupt the speaker without shutting them down. You can do this by validating their participation so they don't feel bad about having shared, but at the same time create space for other learners.

**Counter:** Use your proximity, eye contact, and direct language to invite people of color into the conversation. Keep a mental, color-conscious tally of who has spoken.

**Counter:** Don't always call on the first person to raise their hand in a discussion. Acknowledge a white person who has spoken frequently and the fact that you are not going to call on them: "Greg, I see your hand, but we've heard quite a bit from you already. I'd like to invite some other voices into the conversation for more diversity of perspectives."

**Counter:** "I appreciate how much you have been willing to share with us today. I'm a verbal processor, too (if that's true). I'd like/I need to give those who haven't shared the opportunity to offer their thoughts."

**Counter:** You've noticed a couple of people dominating the conversation in the large group, and you're about to ask the group another question. Before anyone speaks, say, "Let's hear from some new voices."

**Counter:** When a participant who has dominated the conversation starts to open up and share again, you can gracefully put your hand up, move into close proximity, and say, "Hold on, Sheila, I want to first give others the opportunity to share," or "I would like to hear from those who haven't had a chance to share yet," or "Thank you, Sheila, for being willing to take risks and share your thoughts about ____. I'd like to hear from those who have not spoken yet." Allow wait time for others to speak. This may require sitting in silence.

**Counter:** Name dominating the conversation as part of socialization: "As a white person, I always felt like I needed to lead a group or talk a lot. I also know I tend to pay more attention to what men say than what women say because I've been socialized to believe white people and men are more important or better leaders. Has anyone else noticed this tendency in themselves?"

**Counter:** With a group that has some understanding of white privilege, talk directly about this: "I notice you've spoken quite a bit today, Teresa. Given the topic of privilege and power, think about how your identity as a white woman might be playing a role. I encourage you to reflect on why you feel compelled to share. One strategy I use is asking myself: 'WAIT—Why am I talking?'"

## SUGGESTIONS

1. Encourage participants to monitor their own participation and airtime. Some people use the language "Step Up/Step Back."
2. After a small group discussion, ask people to reflect on the group dynamics: "What did you notice about how you participated, who led the group, who spoke first, who asked the most questions? What does this have to do with your conversations about privilege and power?"

# Chapter Twenty-One

## Reframing or Invalidating Experiences of People of Color

Reframing or invalidating experiences of people of color happens when a white participant corrects what a person of color says by restating it through their own lens. They may also imply the person of color is making more of race in the situation than is really true. Often, participants don't realize this is what they are doing. It is usually intended in a helpful way in hopes the person of color will see things in a more positive light. Reframing typically takes this sort of form: "I don't think Mr. Wilson is racist; he's like that with everyone," or "When I go shopping, I'm followed, too." However, the impact of these statements is people of color who have just shared their experiences feel like they are not being heard or believed. They may feel pressure to prove their experience with more evidence, or they may shut down.

White supremacy culture teaches that the white way of experiencing the world is "normal," but people of color have experiences labeled exotic, unusual, or simply not true. It is important for workshop participants to understand white experiences and culture as one way of being in the world, without evaluating different perspectives by centering white norms.

### FACILITATOR'S ROLE

Help the white participant understand how people of color experience the world differently because of racism and create an environment where people of color can share experiences without having their interpretations reframed to fit dominant norms. Push the speaker to reflect on the person of color's experiences.

**Counter:** Have participants suspend their disbelief: "What if that was the case, as Angela describes it; how would that make you feel?"

**Counter:** Use a personal experience to elaborate on the idea of privilege: "We interpret our experiences in different ways. Often, our experiences are based on the privileges that we hold in society. For example, my husband, who has dark skin and is over six feet five, experiences the world differently than I do as a light skinned, short woman. The purpose of the workshop today is to gain insight on how people experience the world differently so we can broaden our perspectives to include other people's experiences."

**Counter:** Tie in norms: "This is an opportunity to listen for understanding."

**Counter:** "It sounds like you want Michael to know he's not alone, that Mr. Wilson treats everyone that way. Sometimes people feel more alone when we don't fully listen to how they experience the world."

**Counter:** "On what do we base our reality and understanding of the world?" (Looking for response of past experiences.) "Past experiences don't have to be our own. They can also be historical experiences of people who look like us, and collective experiences made up of the experiences of family members, friends, and community. These past experiences shape our reality and form our perceptions of how we see the world and, therefore, the way in which we interact with others. How do you think the differences in your past experiences are shaping the way you hear each other's stories?"

**Counter:** Talk about the "mental labor" people of color do on a daily basis. Mental labor is the act of constantly interpreting a white person's words and actions, because of past experiences of racism and discrimination based on skin color.

**Counter:** Name white privilege directly: "Remember when we were talking about how white experiences are 'normalized'? Because of this, it is often hard for a white person to believe a person of color when they are sharing an experience with racism. We may want to think racism isn't that common because that would mean there is more oppression in the world than what we were aware of. Why is it particularly difficult and particularly important to listen for understanding when your experiences have been normalized?"

## SUGGESTIONS

- During these times, you might ask the person of color if you can respond instead, thus removing any burden of proof they may feel about defending their experiences. This allows you to address the bigger issues that need to be discussed, and you can facilitate the conversation between them by being intentional in the direction you want to go and moving through the process slowly. However, if you are using this strategy, be aware of people's desire to speak for themselves, and make sure to ask permission. White facilitators, in particular, may run into resistance if it appears they are attempting to reframe or speak for people of color.
- Navigate the conversation between both people involved. (See chapter 28, "Facilitating Dialogue between Two Participants," for how to navigate a conversation between two participants.)
- Engage the white person to see if you can help them gain insight into how the person of color may have experienced their attempts to be helpful.
- Acknowledge to the audience and to the white participant that you understand, based on what they shared, that their intentions were good before helping them to see the impact it might have had.
- Check in with the person of color and see how they experienced what was said.

## STOP AND REFLECT

1. What are some examples of things you've heard people say that invalidate your own or another person's experience?
2. What ideas do you have to counteract their statements in a way that learning can occur for everyone involved?

_____

_____

_____

_____

_____

_____

_____

_____

_____

# Chapter Twenty-Two

## Valuing the Product over the Process

Valuing the product over the process happens most often in workshops on personal awareness, where participants are required to look deep within themselves. Common statements include, "Why can't we just move on," or "We keep talking about it, but I need strategies," and "I just need to know what to do."

By asking to move on to strategies, the participant is often avoiding the difficult personal work involved in acknowledging, coming to terms with, and consciously countering his or her own biases. Although it is important for adult learners to connect their learning to real situations, coming to new awareness takes time and goes beyond an intellectual exercise to access deep underlying feelings and beliefs. Keeping the focus on strategies before doing awareness work is like learning to dive before learning to swim. You might put on a wonderfully graceful show in the air, but when you hit the water, you quickly go under.

### FACILITATOR'S ROLE

Help participants understand there are no easy recipes in this work. The more aware we are of our own biases, stereotypes, values, attitudes, and beliefs, and the more knowledge we develop of diverse groups, the more likely we are to develop skills that help us to effectively work across cultures. People are too complex to have a one-size-fits-all approach. Those asking for skills are usually the participants who need to do awareness work the most.

**Counter:** "I appreciate your eagerness to learn skills to effectively work across cultures, but that can only happen when you are aware of your own biases, values, and communication styles. It is important first to increase your awareness of self and knowledge of the specific groups with whom you work."

**Counter:** "Unfortunately, this is one of those areas where there are no easy answers. There's not a cookbook that tells us how to work with people given the complexity of individuals and groups. However, if you are willing to do the work of looking at yourself as a racial being and of increasing your knowledge of others, I guarantee it will increase your ability to effectively work across cultures."

**Counter:** Share a story of a mistake you made trying out skills before you had increased your awareness and knowledge. For example, "I once tried to teach a unit on slavery to a middle school class because I thought this was an important, social justice strategy for them to learn African-American history. I didn't have enough awareness or knowledge to talk about context, resistance, or using 'people who were enslaved' instead of 'slaves.' My own biases showed up in the ways I treated the students. Then I was surprised when they called me racist."

**Counter:** Give an example of how awareness and knowledge lead to skills: "If I'm aware that I value eye contact and I have knowledge that a person I'm interacting with sees direct eye contact as a sign of disrespect, I will not expect eye contact from them nor will I judge them based on my norms, particularly if I am in a position of power, such as a teacher to a student. This is one of the ways awareness and knowledge actually grow our skills."

**Counter:** "As I mentioned at the beginning of this workshop, the purpose of today is to focus on increasing awareness of self as it relates to _____."

**Counter:** "What I am hearing from you is that it is important for you to be able to leave with some strategies. Can you think of some things that were shared and discussed today that might help you in developing effective skills?" If they struggle, ask the larger group.

## SUGGESTIONS

- Have them draw a circle with names of people and institutions where they have influence. Ask them to brainstorm: *What things are within your control? What is in your circle of influence?*
- It's good to have a couple of skills or strategies for participants at the end. You can also have them form small groups and come up with their own strategies based on their role within their organization by asking them to respond to a question, such as, *How does what we learned today apply to the work you do?*
- Briefly emphasize how we have become a society wanting quick fixes. State that you don't have any quick fixes, but refer them to resources that will help them.
- Ask them about specific strategies they are looking for. It is much easier to help come up with strategies if you know specific situations they are dealing with.
- Put it back on them: "Let's think about this for a minute. Where do you think you can have the biggest impact in your life? What personal strengths do you bring to this work?"
- Explore what they mean by "tell me what to do." This can help to get at the complexity of this work.

## STOP AND REFLECT

1. What are some other situations where whites value product over process? What do they tend to say and how might you counter their statements?
2. Practice using some of these or your own counteracting statements with a partner.
3. Discuss how the conversation felt. Did your responses shut them down or encourage them to reflect deeper?

_____

_____

_____

_____

_____

_____

_____

_____

_____

_____

_____

_____

_____

_____

# Chapter Twenty-Three

## The Idea That Logic, Reasoning, and Linear Thinking Do Not Involve Emotion

The real art of conversation is not only to say the right thing at the right place but to leave unsaid the wrong thing at the tempting moment.

—Dorothy Nevill

The movie *The Color of Fear* (1994) provides a useful example to illustrate this expression of privilege. At one point, Victor Lee Lewis, an African-American man, was angry and also very logical and clear about what he was saying. He wasn't out of control. However, for some people the anger and their associated stereotypes prevent them from seeing the logic. This can be conveyed by a white person telling a person of color to calm down or, at the beginning of the day, requesting the workshop be "safe" for them.

### FACILITATOR'S ROLE

Allow participants to express a diverse range of emotions and create a space where learning can occur with the emotion present in the room. Be aware of your own reactions to crying, speaking loudly, and silence. Be ready to name tension and have participants reflect on their feelings and reactions to what transpired in the room.

**Counter:** "What does 'safe' mean to you?"

**Counter:** "What's going on in your mind at this moment, when you hear Lisa express her thoughts with so much emotion?"

**Counter:** "How were you taught to express emotion?" You may be able to name the emotion exhibited, such as anger, but this can create defensive feelings if you identify the wrong emotion. It is better to identify the behavior, such as raising the voice, and then ask what the participant is feeling.

**Counter:** "Which emotions were you allowed to express or taught not to express growing up? What does dominant culture tell us about expressing emotions?"

**Counter:** "Take a moment to stop and reflect on what was going on for you when we engaged in courageous conversations for the past 15 minutes. How were you taught to communicate, and how did that impact how you showed up in the room?"

**Counter:** "What is the benefit of seeing the emotions involved in these issues? What do we miss if we just stay in our heads?"

## SUGGESTIONS

- Tie in how stereotypes often interfere with our ability to appropriately assess our reactions to different emotions. For example, a common stereotype for African-American men is that they are aggressive or dangerous. Frequently whites, particularly white women, become very uncomfortable, even fearful, when they are in the presence of an African-American person expressing how they feel. This fear can be evident even when African Americans don't show emotion. Help white participants explore where they have received messages about African Americans. This can aid them in discerning the validity of their fear and also affirm the very real anger many African Americans feel about their experiences of racism. There is a difference between "an angry black man" and "a black man who is angry."
- Whenever possible, talk about the here and now— what's happening in the room at that very moment.

## STOP AND REFLECT

1. How do you feel when others become emotional—angry, tearful, frustrated, and so on?
2. Which emotion(s) makes you feel the most uncomfortable and why?
3. What were you taught about expressing emotions growing up?

# Chapter Twenty-Four

## Being Agenda-Bound

An expert is a man who has made all the mistakes, which can be made, in a very narrow field.

—Neils Bohr

When we conduct workshops on privilege and oppression, we are looking for opportunities to deepen and broaden people's perspectives. Activities are just stimuli to get participants to engage. If the conversation is engaging participants in a meaningful way, it may not be necessary to do the planned activity. Make sure you identify your goals prior to beginning so you can make thoughtful decisions as issues come up.

When an opportunity arises, the skilled facilitator can recognize something important is happening and abandon some planned activities. Educators call this a "teachable moment." It may happen in the form of heightened emotions, engaged dialogue in small groups, or a critical question being raised.

Similar to valuing product over process, being agenda-bound may relieve members of dominant groups from the duty to closely examine themselves as they try to use the posted agenda as an avoidance strategy. Participants want to focus on the agenda and move forward in a linear fashion, rather than seeing the value of diving into tension. At the same time, keep in mind that, culturally, whites tend to be linear in their thinking, so don't assume too quickly they are avoiding the conversation.

Common ways this may show up include statements like these: "Are we going to watch that video you mentioned?" or "I thought we were going to talk about ____."

## FACILITATOR'S ROLE

Take the conversation to deeper levels of learning. You have to be flexible by moving away from the schedule of the day. Assess and see what is working best for the entire group, not just one individual. There is a risk here of catering to the person who has the least understanding going into the workshop. Because you want to help everyone grow their understanding, it is also important to be conscious of time spent "reeducating" one person.

**Counter:** State in the beginning of the workshop, "The agenda is a tool to guide us in the direction we are going in. If something else takes us to the outcome we are trying to achieve today, I may facilitate us down a different path than what was originally planned. I know that this is not something that everyone feels comfortable with, depending on their learning styles, but I am going to ask you to trust you will get what I intended for you to receive today, regardless of whether we cover everything."

**Counter:** "When something difficult comes up, we're going to sit in the fire and wrestle with it. Sometimes it's important to stay with the here and now rather than stick to the agenda."

## SUGGESTIONS

- Don't post break times or lunch times in your agenda for participants. This allows you to be more flexible without people "checking out" because of when they think breaks are supposed to happen.
- Have participants take a moment to explore how their learning is relevant to their personal and professional lives.
- Briefly talk about the different needs and styles of learning.
- Help the agenda-bound participant explore their anxiety around "missing out" on something that was planned but is not being covered for the sake of focusing on the here and now. Consider ways you can include their experience and resistance in the dialogue.

# Chapter Twenty-Five

## Whites Distancing Themselves from Other Whites

This often occurs in the form of white people criticizing other white people for comments they make. There is a sense of superiority in the tone. It feels as though they are saying, "You don't understand what I have come to understand about these issues." Underneath there can be shame, guilt, and embarrassment about one's own whiteness that comes off as aggression towards other whites who are early in their development of racial cognizance. We once had a white male participant in a workshop point out that whites are so used to being seen as superior that even when they take on the identity of white ally they can unconsciously see that role from a superior perspective. In other words, they are constantly putting themselves in the position of being better than someone else.

### FACILITATOR'S ROLE

Unpack the issues between white people. The goal is not to shame people into understanding, but rather to guide them from where they are to new understanding. We don't want to lose our allies but, rather, help them to better understand their behavior so they can be more effective in their work.

**Counter:** Point out the behavior that you see occurring: "Michelle, I noticed that you have responded three times to the comments of other white people in the room. Did you notice that? Where do you think that's coming from?"

**Counter:** "I see you as someone committed to this work. Throughout this workshop you have been engaged and willing to take risks. So, I'm going to trust that you can engage on a deeper level. I've noticed that when white people in the room speak up, you respond with a comment on something they missed or don't understand. What is going on for you as you hear white people speaking? What is it that you want for us to understand or know about you?"

### SUGGESTIONS

- Start out with an authentic compliment or something positive.
- Try to get to the deeper issue that may be occurring, for example, embarrassment, shame, or disassociation, that is, "I don't want people to see me as someone like you."

- If they struggle with responding, name what you think might be going on. For example, "In most of the Identity Development Models, they mention a person experiencing shame and embarrassment towards their own ethnic group. Do you think this might be something that is occurring for you today?"
- Normalize their feelings. Suggest that what's important is that participants identify what they are experiencing and work towards alleviating those feelings. These feelings are normal, but it's not a good place to stay. Feelings of shame, guilt, and embarrassment become barriers to our growth and the growth of others.
- Try to get them to empathize with where the other person is at. This can be done by helping them to recall a time when they thought that way.
- When closing the conversation, acknowledge the difficulty of the work and praise everyone—observers and participants—in their willingness to stay with it.
- Praise the person you assisted in going deeper by identifying their strengths in handling the conversation: "Michael, this was very difficult work. Many people would have shut down, but you didn't. Good work! How are you feeling about what just occurred?"

# Chapter Twenty-Six

## Either/Or Thinking

Shared pain is no longer paralyzing but mobilizing, when understood as a way to liberation. When we become aware that we do not have to escape our pains, but that we can mobilize them into a common search for life, those very pains are transformed from expressions of despair into signs of hope. Through this common search, hospitality becomes community. Hospitality becomes community as it creates a unity based on the shared confession of our basic brokenness and on a shared hope.

—Henri J. M. Nouwen

White supremacy culture teaches us to think in dichotomies. Facilitators or participants may demonstrate this by talking about issues of race in terms of only black and white, good or bad, with us or against us. Because we see racism as bad, it is difficult for us to acknowledge our own biases because that would make us racist, and therefore bad.

The tendency to label people as one way or another leaves little room for learning or growth, much less the range and complexity of our experiences and opinions. Psychologists refer to this as the "Halo Effect." Once we've decided we either like or don't like someone, we generalize that opinion to all of their behaviors, offering them more space for disagreement and learning when they are on the "angel" side, and quickly dismissing them when they fall into our "devil" category.

Either/or thinking also limits our capacity for creative solutions. As a result, addressing issues of privilege and power may seem insurmountable.

### FACILITATOR'S ROLE

See the beauty in all participants, especially when you disagree with something they've said early on or if they remind you of someone you dislike. Help participants recognize when they are judging themselves or others as good or bad. Name either/or thinking when it surfaces in conversations and ask about other options.

**Counter:** "It seems like this conversation has mostly centered around issues of black and white. This happens often when talking about race, and we fail to see the full complexity of race issues. What are other experiences or perspectives that don't fall into the black/white dichotomy?"

**Counter:** "Tamara, I noticed you've mentioned seeing people you don't like doing racist things. Have you ever had a friend or family member that did something racist, but you still cared about that person?" (Let her respond.) "Why do you think it is more difficult to talk about those experiences?"

**Counter:** "What I'm hearing right now is either/or thinking. That's one of the dynamics that keeps white privilege in place. What other possibilities lie on the spectrum between (this point of view) and (the opposite one)?"

**Counter:** "Instead of saying, 'yes, but,' let's say, 'yes, and.' This can help get us out of thinking of issues as just being two-sided."

By identifying and counteracting expressions of white privilege in workshops, all participants come to a deeper understanding of cross-cultural dynamics. This builds our skills so we can engage in more authentic conversations about what is being communicated, both through what is not said and what is said. Because of the nature of white privilege, even the most skilled facilitators will still have participants who shut down or walk out of the room. The goal is not to make everyone feel comfortable; it is to allow people the space to experience the discomfort that comes from realizing the world is not as they had thought, while not using oppressive tools of shame and guilt to try to force new learning. These strategies help us bridge racial divides and create cross-cultural connections.

## STOP AND REFLECT

1. Identify 1 to 3 different unearned privileges you have (e.g., race, class, gender, sexual orientation, age, religion, ability, etc.).
2. In what ways do you benefit from those privileges in your personal and professional life?

# SECTION V

# FACILITATING COURAGEOUS CONVERSATIONS

In the face of diversity, we feel tension—and that, in turn, can lead to discomfort, distrust, conflict, violence, and even war. So we have developed a variety of strategies to evade our differences, strategies that only deepen our fear, such as associating exclusively with "our own kind" or using one of our well-tested methods to dismiss, marginalize, demonize, or eliminate the stranger. When our ancient fear of otherness is left unacknowledged, unattended, and untreated, diversity creates dysfunctional communities. The benefits of diversity can be ours only if we hold our differences with respect, patience, openness, and hope, which means we must attend to the invisible dynamics of the heart that are part of democracy's infrastructure.

—Parker Palmer

# Chapter Twenty-Seven

## Strategies for Facilitating Courageous Conversations

When I ask open questions, I assume folks have some neat thoughts of their own, that they can do something other than regurgitate facts, and that what they have to say is valuable. When I ask open questions, I energize learners' minds and help them focus.

—Dr. Joye Norris

*Brilliant responses that rock a person's world and get them to think more deeply about the issues don't usually come to you until you drive home. That's okay, though. The universe will give you another chance.*

Given the history of race relations in this country, facilitating conversations on race is challenging, even for the most seasoned facilitator. Denial, fear, anger, despair, grief, and frustration are just a few emotions that facilitators will have to steer participants through so they can embrace the truth about racism, let go of seeing one another as enemies, and work together for social change.

Even without the emotions people bring into the room, it can be S-C-A-R-Y to have so many people watching your every move and waiting to see how you will handle controversy. Though you only have a few brief moments to respond, it is somehow enough time for self-doubt to settle in. You can quickly become consumed with questions like, "How do I handle this in the best way? Should I try to address this at all?" And then there are those immobilizing questions that bombard you: "What will happen if I address this?" Followed by, "What if I make things worse? What if I cause more harm? What if someone gets hurt? What if things get out of control? What if people become too emotional? What if they don't like me? What if, what if, what if ?!!!" All of this uncertainty can wreak havoc on your mind, causing you to panic and paralyzing you from grabbing hold of the situation. And still, people are watching.

Consider that many people of color feel uncomfortable at the expense of white people's comfort every day. When conversations become tense, the false assumption is often made that the tension didn't exist until you brought it up. In reality, the tension has always been there; it's just not talked about between groups. Ask yourself repeatedly in these conversations: Whose interests are being served when we don't have these conversations? And if not me, then who will help us to talk about it?

The key is to dive into the tension, rather than back off and avoid discomfort. Strategies mentioned earlier in this book combined with others shared in this section will help prepare you for some of the toughest situations you will face. Reading about it is not enough. In order to navigate participants through these choppy waters, you will have to resist giving in to your fears, take risks, and practice sitting in the fire. When tension and emotion are in the room, those can be some of the greatest opportunities for learning. Remember this is a process, and you will learn through your successes and mistakes.

## WHEN SOMEONE SAYS SOMETHING THAT CAUSES TENSION TO RISE IN THE ROOM

While you may be able to control what you say and do, you will never be able to control what comes out of the mouths of participants. When you set the norms at the beginning of the workshop by inviting participants to speak their truth, many will do just that. While it may be anxiety-provoking the moment a controversial statement is made, the tension needs to be revealed in order for us to reconcile our differences. Therefore, it's essential you move participants into rather than away from courageous conversations. Here are several strategies to encourage a participant who has offended to engage in spite of the discomfort.

### *Get permission from the participant who made the comment.*

A lot of attention will be placed on one participant in the room, and it will increase his or her anxiety to a greater degree than anyone else's. While we have never had someone who verbally stated they were unwilling to engage, it is still necessary to ask their consent so they don't feel forced into it. It also shows you care when you first ask permission before diving in to a large group discussion.

Example:

1. After Mike makes the comment, move in close to him, touch him on the shoulder if you think it is appropriate (you have connected with him in some way earlier or he seems open to touch).
2. "Mike, when you were talking about youth and how it's important for you to see them all the same rather than notice racial differences, did you pick up on the change in the room?"
3. Let Mike respond. If he says no, share with him what you noticed.
4. Whether he replied yes or no, ask him, "Would you be open to hearing what your comments triggered in some of your colleagues?

5. If he says yes, then thank him: "I appreciate your willingness to take a risk."

6. If he says no, speak to him while at the same time addressing the entire group. You want to convey understanding of his decision not to involve the whole group, and encourage him to continue to discuss this later: "I can imagine that it would be scary to get feedback in this way and feel put on the spot. I believe you could learn a lot and grow in your understanding of race relations by hearing from your colleagues. However, I respect your decision to not do this in such a public manner. And so, if you are willing, Mike, I'd like for you to challenge yourself and at the very least talk to 2 or 3 people during the break, particularly if there is anyone you noticed was affected by your comment. Ask them what your comment triggered in them. Is that something you can see yourself doing?"

7. Then let it go.

8. If he says yes, turn to the group, and ask 2 or 3 people: "I, too, noticed a change in the room. Would someone be willing to share what the comment triggered in them? Keep in mind as you share how difficult this is to be in Mike's seat right now. Our goal is to help him understand."

9. Compliment individuals that share for their willingness to give of themselves so that another person could deepen their own understanding. Learning how to share their thoughts is also a part of their growth.

10. Circle back around to Mike by asking a question that will give him the opportunity to share what he is hearing and/or understanding: "Mike, what are you hearing from your colleagues? Are there any questions you have for them?"

11. Praise Mike for being willing to take risk and experience discomfort.

### Point out what is happening in the room in the moment.

- This is a reminder to participants that these conversations are difficult, and what is happening is not a bad thing. It can also help ease your own anxiety by reminding you of the importance of diving in rather than avoiding the conversation.

  - *What we are doing now is what Glenn Singleton refers to as courageous conversations. I know it's not easy, but let's try and stay in it.*

  - *Given the tension that's in the room right now, how can we stay engaged and continue to work through this difficult conversation?*

  - *This may feel difficult, but these are the kinds of discussions we usually have about, rather than with, one another. Talking about it today gives us the opportunity to build community, and practice effectively engaging, even as it may feel easier to avoid our deep divisions.*

### Have participants name their feelings and talk about their reactions.

- Asking a few participants to talk about what is coming up for them acknowledges that people are having a reaction to what was said, and that it needs to be addressed rather than swept under the carpet.

  - *How did hearing ____make you feel?*

  - *When you heard ____, what feelings came up for you?*

- *I felt something just happen in the room, what's going on for people?*

- *Let's pause for a moment and talk about what people are thinking and feeling. Would anyone be willing to take a risk and share their thoughts and feelings as a result of what was just said?*

- *I'm wondering if anyone had an emotional reaction to what was just said?*

- *This is one of those times where speaking your truth is important so we can talk about what is happening in the room. Would anyone be willing to take a risk and share what's going on for them?*

- *It feels like there is tension in the room related to Anthony's comment. Remember one of our norms is to "experience discomfort." Would anyone be willing to take a risk and share your reactions?*

- *I'm feeling tension in the room right now; am I the only one or do others feel it too?*

### Remind them of the norms to "normalize" what's happening in the moment.

- Norms can be used at any point and any time in the conversation but are particularly helpful during those challenging moments when you want to remind them what is happening is to be expected.

  - *Remember, it's important that we "listen for understanding." Barbara, what do you hear Anita saying?*

  - *It's hard to become comfortable with the discomfort having these conversations elicits in us. Remember it is a norm when talking about race.*

  - *I'm going to ask everyone to stay engaged.*

  - *I'm going stop us here, keeping in mind the norm "expect and accept nonclosure."*

### Encourage courageous conversations among participants.

- You can encourage participants to stay engaged by using general statements throughout the discourse. There will be moments when things become so difficult you will want to give up, and so will they. Guiding participants along the way can be a helpful strategy in keeping the conversation going.

  - *I can appreciate the difficulty of this conversation, but even more so the way people are being thoughtful in how they convey their feelings to one another.*

  - *I want to remind everyone that people have different styles of communicating. It's important we listen for understanding.*

  - *Remember, we are all in different places in our racial/ethnic identity development. If we want to help one another grow, we have to be willing to support each other by meeting people where they are at, otherwise we risk shutting the conversation down.*

  - *I have never led a group this deep into courageous conversation, and I have to admit this is hard for me, too. It speaks to your uniqueness as a group, and I want to remind you that it's important we all step outside of our comfort zones and take risks.*

- *Thank you for staying with this conversation, given how difficult it is.*

- *I can feel the tension rising in the room, and I want to remind people this is a normal part of the work. Let's see if we can stay with our discomfort.*

- *What do others think about what was said?*

- *Has anyone else had the same thoughts/feelings Carlos just described?*

- *In the United States, we hear that point of view quite a bit. Why do you think that is such a popular idea?*

- *I hear that a lot. How did you personally come to that understanding? Do others have a different view?*

- *Given what we know about the racial divide between who is wealthy and who is poor in this country, what would that perspective lead us to believe about white people? About people of color?*

### *Encourage participants to be open to new learning.*

- Statements that remind everyone that to develop our cultural competence, we have to be open to new learning are helpful, particularly during those moments when you feel the conversation is becoming more difficult.

  - *I appreciate Lynn bringing this up because she is touching on something that a lot of people feel but are often afraid to say. We can't have courageous conversations if people aren't willing to take risks and share their thinking.*

  - *The only way we can learn is to share our thoughts and be willing to hear and be open to feedback about our thinking.*

  - *Remember that one way to grow in this work is to engage one another in conversations. We have to be willing to listen for understanding.*

### *Thank the participant who made the comment.*

- Even though you will be engaging the entire group, the participant who made the statement is likely to feel a deeper level of discomfort. It's difficult to keep them engaged when they feel put on the spot. Praising them throughout the conversation and at the end can help them to stay with it.

  - *How are you doing, Angela? I don't want to lose you in this conversation. Thank you for staying with us so far.*

  - *I imagine it's difficult to be in your shoes in this moment. I appreciate your courage and willingness to ride through this tension.*

  - *I want to thank you, Sharon, for sticking with the conversation, particularly at the most difficult times. What you said triggered a lot of reaction in the room, but what I appreciate most was your willingness to stay engaged so we could move forward as a group.*

- *Thank you, Justin. I imagine that wasn't easy for you to stay present, but by not dropping out emotionally you allowed us to work through some very difficult conversations. That's what it means to engage in courageous conversations.*

### Thank everyone in the room for their participation.

- Everyone has contributed in some way or another to the conversation. Thank them for challenging themselves to engage, and point out some of the things they did well.
  - *This was difficult, and I want to thank you for staying with it.*
  - *I appreciate the way you addressed what Larry said without stomping on his head.*
  - *It wasn't easy for any of us to have this conversation, but I like the way we are listening for understanding.*
  - *Dean, you really put yourself out there when you shared your story. Thank you for caring enough about Leslie and these issues to give of yourself in vulnerable ways.*
  - *Nice work everyone. I noticed that you didn't try and shame, blame, or guilt Heidi into understanding your perspectives.*
  - *Thank you for sharing something so personal about yourself. For some people, that's not an easy thing to do.*
  - *Let's give Dan a round of applause for taking a risk, listening for understanding, and—what I would imagine—experiencing "extreme" discomfort. Let's also give ourselves a round of applause for practicing engagement strategies that open up the dialogue.*

We are always hopeful of a breakthrough with the participant who made the comment. It would be wonderful if as a result of our facilitation they had an epiphany. Sometimes this happens, but not always. Sometimes the conversation falls flat. This doesn't mean it wasn't a success. You have modeled for participants what it means to effectively engage. They have learned they can weather the storm, and they probably left with a few bruises—though not broken bones, or spirits. And you are on your way to becoming a more skilled facilitator.

# Chapter Twenty-Eight

## Facilitating Dialogue between Two Participants

The need to facilitate dialogue between two participants can happen when there is an exchange of words that results in verbal or nonverbal discord. This commonly occurs when a white participant reveals something a person of color has a negative reaction to. This is an opportunity for the facilitator to demonstrate conflict resolution.

The process is slow and involves several steps by the facilitator. First, you will need to find out if the participant realizes their words were offensive. Often the person who makes the comment has no idea of the impact of their words. Second, you will need to get both parties to agree to talk about it. In many ways this approach is perfunctory. When participants are put on the spot and asked if they are willing to engage one another, they are likely to say yes. They're both at your workshop to grow in their understanding of race relations and, as such, may feel that saying no would reveal their resistance to change. However, asking permission honors their right to choose.

Third, and by far the most difficult, you will need to navigate the conversation between the two of them. This will require a great deal of strength and confidence on your part. You will need to support both people so they feel you are not taking sides, control the direction of the conversation so that it doesn't go off task, and interrupt at any given moment to invite participants to reflect on what they are feeling and experiencing. How and when to do what is difficult to say. It will all depend on the situation and the people involved. Listen carefully to what is said and not said. Watch body language. Your objective is to facilitate the conversation so participants engage one another rather than attack or avoid. There is definitely no formulaic approach to this process, but we have provided you with the following example to get an idea of how this might unfold.

Example:

1. "It seems like what was said really upset you, Nina (person of color). If it's okay with you and Jeff (white person who triggered response), I'd like to see if I can assist the two of you in engaging one another in courageous conversations. Would that be all right with you?"

**Note**: Stand near the person you are addressing but check in with the other person through eye contact. This often means you will have to walk back and forth between the two participants or ask someone to exchange seats so that they are sitting in closer proximity. You will want to make sure you get affirmation from both parties before moving forward. We have never experienced the person of color refusing. They are usually eager to be able to talk about what is going on for them.

2. "Thank you, Nina. I appreciate your willingness to be put on the spot and letting me help guide you through this process."
3. "Jeff, did you even realize what you were saying might be offensive to someone in the room or that it might trigger an emotional reaction like it did?"

**Note**: He's likely to say no. Most people don't intend to harm or say insensitive things. Remember that you are having this workshop so you and others grow in their understanding. You may even want to say something to this effect to the entire group. You also want to ask a question of this type so participants in the room don't see him as the enemy.

4. "Would you be willing to hear from Nina what she reacted to and why?"

**Note**: In the majority of cases, the person in Jeff's shoes will say yes. But if he says no, ask him what he is feeling at the moment, try to get at his fears. If he says no, you can also ask if it would be okay to talk about situations that commonly occur like this one with the entire group. This approach takes the spotlight off him and recognizes that he is not the only one who makes offensive remarks. If this happens, address the entire group in a way that brings understanding for why Jeff would not want to engage one-on-one. Anyone could be terrified to be put in this situation.

5. (Addressing everyone if Jeff says yes) "Thank you, Jeff, for your willingness to engage. I want to pause for a moment and acknowledge this is an example of how conflict can occur across cultures. Oftentimes, when someone says something with good intentions, they have no awareness it was offensive. The person who was offended may attack or avoid the conversation, but rarely does she know how to effectively engage. We simply do not get enough practice at it. As a result, the person offended is left to deal with their feelings on their own, possibly in unhealthy or ineffective ways. They may find it difficult to mentally move forward with whatever is happening in the room, in this case, the content of this workshop, because they are stuck with the offensive comment rolling around in their head. At the same time, the person who offended has no clue what has just happened. If it's not addressed, they lose the opportunity to grow in their understanding. This may or may not be true for Nina and Jeff, but we do have an opportunity to have them engage in a commonly occurring situation, so we can all learn how to talk about these experiences more effectively. This is what you all came here for, right?"
6. "Thank you, Nina, for taking a risk to express your reactions to Jeff. And thank you both for being willing to try something out with me."
7. "Nina, would you please say more about what you reacted to, and, as you do, turn around so you can speak directly to Jeff. Tell him what you heard him saying."

**Note**: This is one place where you may need to interrupt. Nina may be filled with uncensored emotion, in which case it might feel to Jeff as though he is being attacked. Or she could avoid being direct, so much so that Jeff becomes unclear about how what he said offended.

If the first is true, ask her if she could restate what she just said, but in a way that Jeff would be open to hearing. At the same time, validate her feelings. For example, "Nina, I'm guessing the comment Jeff made really impacted you on a deep level. When someone says something offensive, we are reacting not just to the one time it was said by one individual but all of the times it was said by many different people. I'm sensing a lot of feelings coming from you. I don't want to invalidate those feelings, and at the same time I'm worried that Jeff won't be able to hear your words. Is there a way you could restate what you said in a way that would be more inviting to Jeff to engage?"

If the latter is true, you can help Nina by naming what you think might be going on for her and then check in with her for accuracy. "Nina, I'm sensing that you are being very careful not to push Jeff away from this conversation. I may be projecting here, but I sometimes worry that if I come off too strong, I will lose the person in the conversation and therefore lose a potential ally. However, I want to make sure Jeff is clear about what happened between the two of you so he can grow in his understanding. What I'm picking up from you is that you were upset when he said _____ because it conveys _____. Am I accurately communicating what you were trying to say?" You could also ask Nina to restate what she was trying to say rather than you doing it for her.

8. "Jeff, would you share with us what you hear Nina saying about why she reacted to what you said?"

**Note**: At this point, your goal is to make sure that Jeff is clear regarding what offended Nina, before moving forward. Stop this part of the conversation once Jeff conveys understanding. This might take several times of going back and forth between them. The process involves having Jeff summarize what he is hearing Nina say, and then checking in with Nina to affirm that Jeff understood her correctly. "Nina, is Jeff capturing what you are trying to say?" If Jeff is still having trouble understanding after going back and forth several times, you may have to elicit support from the larger group and invite others to talk with Jeff about what upset Nina.

If Jeff tries to explain his intentions rather than sit with the impact, interrupt and redirect until he shows understanding of what Nina is saying. This can be challenging because he is likely to be feeling embarrassed or ashamed. In these situations, people struggle with others having an image of them as "bad" in any way. Their aim becomes to correct that image as soon as possible, making it difficult to sit in the tension and listen to the impact of their words. They will try to easily "fix" the situation by stating what they "meant" or quickly apologizing, rather than listening for understanding of the impact. Don't let him focus on intent. At this point you just want to know he hears the impact of his words. You may have to tell him you will give him an opportunity to speak later, but for right now you just want to be sure he understands what Nina was reacting to. It is not uncommon that he will feel some frustration at not being allowed to say what he wants.

9. "Jeff, I know this is hard for you. It would be extremely difficult for anyone in your shoes. You are doing well, but I need you to trust me to guide you through this. My guess is that everyone in this room, including Nina and I, know you did not mean harm when you said what you said. What I'm asking is if you would be willing to sit in the discomfort and hear how what you said impacted Nina. This is the norm 'listen for understanding' I was talking about earlier this morning. I will give you an opportunity later if you still need it, to talk about your intentions."

10. (To Nina) "Nina, does that help at all, what Jeff just said? Where are you now in your thinking or reactions to his earlier comment?"

Once you are able to get Jeff to show that he is listening, the remainder of the process involves checking in with the two of them about their experiences and feelings as they dialogue with one another. It also involves you letting them speak more freely to one another without as many interruptions on your part. Your hope is to get them to dialogue so they are engaging each other effectively. If you only accomplish the first part, listening for understanding, something good has come from it. While this rarely, if ever, has a kumbaya ending, it can leave Nina feeling heard, Jeff with a deeper level of understanding, and participants having learned new strategies for effectively engaging.

11. Always close by honoring the hard work. "Thank you both for modeling risk-taking. I can't imagine it was easy for either of you. I really appreciated your patience, Nina. You showed a great deal of care towards Jeff in this process. And, Jeff, you did an incredible job staying present, particularly when you wanted to explain the intent instead of the impact. I was afraid I was going to lose you in the conversation, but you stuck with it."

When it goes really well, we will sometimes process the experience with the large group to pull out what worked by asking questions like these:

1. What did Jeff do well?
2. What did Nina do well?
3. What were some of the strategies I used to help them effectively engage?

Some other guiding questions/comments that might be helpful in the above situation:

- *Keep in mind that we are all here to learn from each other.*

- *Jeff, as Nina shares with you, you will be in a very difficult situation because it's easier to focus on intent instead of impact. I want you to do your best to think of what she's sharing with you as a gift she is giving to you—something that will help you in the future in conversations.*

- *Nina, have you experienced this before where someone said ____.*

- *Jeff, have you ever been misunderstood in race conversations before? What was that like for you? So then I imagine this is really difficult for you. I appreciate your willingness to take a risk.*

- *When we don't have these conversations with each other, we usually have them in the parking lots or near the water coolers, oftentimes with people who weren't even present. If we want to close the racial divide, we have to practice developing skills of engaging in courageous conversations, sometimes in the moment when we have offended.*

You may want to call for a break. What just happened in the room was intense and everyone is likely to need some time to be with their own thoughts.

The more present you are in the conversation, the more successful you will be. Try to listen without planning what to say or do next, as much as possible.

- Slow the conversation down and take a step by step approach.
- Balance your compliments and questions to both participants. It is common to focus so much on the person who offended that we omit the care needed for the person negatively impacted.
- Help them to paraphrase, summarize, and reframe what they hear the other person saying.
- Make sure they are talking to each other and not to you. You may even ask someone to trade seats so they can be closer together. Sometimes you will need to ask them to look at each other or to speak directly to one another by redirecting their words or eye contact.
- Remind them of specific norms at relevant times.
- If either speaks in an attacking or defensive manner, stop them and ask what is going on for them in the moment. Have them identify feelings, validate those feelings, and then ask them if there is another way they can share what they want the other person to hear.
- Check in periodically to ask where they are at in the moment regarding feelings, thoughts, challenges, and so on.
- Keep your eyes on the audience to make sure they are engaged with what is happening in the room.
- It's difficult to know when to end it. A process like this can take up to 20 or 30 minutes.

Sometimes a participant will say something offensive that you did not pick up on. This can happen for a couple of reasons. One reason is it went over your head. It could also be that you were not offended by the comment and therefore hadn't realized others might have been. Whatever the reason, when this occurs let the group know why you didn't say something. By doing this you are essentially letting them know what offends one person doesn't necessarily offend everyone. It is still necessary that you help the room examine the impact.

# Chapter Twenty-Nine

## Engaging the Resistance

Where race is the subject, talking and listening are forms of action.

—John Noonan

### WHEN SOMEONE RESPONDS NEGATIVELY TO SOMETHING YOU SAID

It can be extremely challenging to be in the front of the room as the facilitator who is supposed to possess a degree of expertise and have someone point out that you have said or done something offensive. However, it is nearly impossible to facilitate conversations on race and not at some point offend people in the process. So be ready. The most important thing to do is own your mistakes publicly and make it a learning opportunity for everyone in the room, including yourself. You can use these times to be a role model by demonstrating your openness to learning, demonstrating effective engagement, handling the discomfort, and showing your willingness to learn from your mistakes.

Once when facilitating a workshop for people who work with people with intellectual and developmental disabilities, I used the term "mental retardation." I knew enough to know that it is insulting to use that language to put people down by making statements like "that's so retarded," but I wasn't aware that the relatively new terminology is "intellectual disability." The moment I said it in a room of more than 50 people, the silence was so thick you could hear a pin drop. I didn't have a lot of experience facilitating workshops with this particular audience and already had a degree of anxiety leading up to it. In this moment, my heart started racing and my mind quickly sifted through what to do. There was really only one thing I could do—talk about it. So I asked the group to raise their hand if I had just said something offensive and then asked them to tell me what it was I had said. I then asked 4 or 5 people to share with me why it was offensive to them and to share their emotional reaction. It ended up being great dialogue, and I was able to reiterate the point that we are all growing in our cultural competence. I thanked them for being open and their willingness to take risks and speak their truth, given my power in the room as a facilitator. I learned much from that workshop, and I now use this as an example in other workshops that I, too, am constantly in the process of growing in my understanding.

## WAYS TO SHOW YOU'RE OPEN TO HEARING AND
## LEARNING FROM PARTICIPANTS

- That's what's great about doing these workshops, I'm always learning about my own unconscious incompetence.
- I appreciate your telling me that because it validates some of the feedback I've received from others.
- I haven't heard that before. I will have to reflect on your comment at a time when I can really think about it. Thank you for sharing your thoughts. I know that sometimes it can be difficult to challenge the facilitator.
- Did anyone else pick up on the same thing Sheila did when I said, "_____."
- For a white facilitator: I appreciate your feedback. Like all of us, I've been socialized with stereotypes and racism. I'm wondering what role my whiteness is playing right now?
- What did I, as the facilitator, represent in this last activity? Do you think that influenced how you were seeing my individual actions?
- Many times, we're more attuned to things that have happened more than once. Do my actions remind you of other experiences you've had?

## WHEN YOU DISAGREE WITH WHAT IS SAID

When participants say things you disagree with, it's important you respond not just so they contemplate another perspective but also so other participants in the room hear alternative viewpoints. You don't have to argue your perception, but you don't want to ignore what was said either. Silence often conveys consent. Here are some simple strategies to broaden perspectives:

*I've also heard people say_____.*
*Linda's approach is to treat all her students the same; what are other people's experiences?*
*I know other people share your same views. Here's what I've come to understand about_____.*
*Does anyone have another perspective on that?*
*I have never heard that before. I know that some people think _____.*
*I have never heard that before. I've read research that says that_____.*
*I've heard many people say that. Does anyone have a different perspective?*
*What are some other thoughts about_____?*

## WHEN YOU ARE NOT SURE HOW TO RESPOND

Sometimes we find ourselves in situations where we aren't quite sure how to respond to a question or comment. Sometimes we don't want participants to know what we don't know.

However, admitting you don't know the answer is a great way to invite others in to share their expertise, and it models your own vulnerability and learning.

When someone directs the question or comment to you and you're not quite sure how to respond, it's perfectly okay to ask other participants in the room to respond simply by stating: "I'm not sure, that's a great question. Does anyone have any thoughts or ideas about ____?"

## WHEN YOU HAVE AN EMOTIONAL REACTION TO WHAT WAS SAID

We are all human. Being a trained facilitator will not make you immune from responding emotionally to what is said by your participants. No matter how much you prepare or how many times you have heard the same emotionally laden comments, there will be days when you are caught off guard by your own reactions. Whether it's something new you hadn't heard before or a familiar comment that hits you the wrong way, you won't always handle it well, even with years of practice or new-found strategies you've equipped yourself with. When things don't go well, be sure to process it with a trusted colleague and give yourself grace.

- *Try to identify why you are reacting strongly to what was said.* One of my worst facilitations moments happened about 6 months ago when a participant made a comment during an activity addressing white privilege. I instantly found my emotions rising up. Initially, I was able to navigate the comment, but after other participants, Ilsa, who was co-facilitating, and I tried to get him to look at it from a different perspective, I found myself becoming angry. His reaction to this exercise was not new to me, but my response was. Anyone in the room could see that I was becoming angry. Something that I am usually good at keeping to myself. As a facilitator you have a lot of power, and when your emotions become too evident, particularly anger, it can scare participants from opening up. Eventually my anger turned to tears, and before I knew it, I had lost all control of my emotions. As a result, I became the focus of the conversation and was no longer able to effectively facilitate. In the moment, I tried to pull it together but was unable to. I couldn't figure out what was going on with me. During the workshop and in days following, I felt immense shame and embarrassment. It took me a week before I fully processed it, and several weeks before I could talk openly to others outside my support circle. I discovered several things that were going on for me, none having to do with the person who triggered my response: (1) I was up late the night before watching a documentary about racism with my husband. Besides not getting the sleep I needed, I believe this unconsciously fueled my angry feelings about institutional racism that I then projected onto the participant; (2) I was experiencing physical changes in my body; and (3) I had received a call from my son's principal that same day about a serious issue he was involved in at school. While I have always known that it is essential facilitators get a good night's sleep so we are sharp and mentally prepared to handle what comes our way, I had never thought before about the impact of what I watch on television or do the night before. The latter two were likely unavoidable, but if I could have done it again, knowing what goes on in my life impacts how I show up as a facilitator, I would have found some time to process out loud with Ilsa. This could have helped bring my unconscious feelings to the surface so both Ilsa and I were prepared rather than blindsided by my outburst.

- *Take a deep breath.* Breathing helps you think more clearly. If necessary and possible, take a quick break and find someplace quiet to think, meditate, or pray. Whatever you do to clear your mind and find focus, do it now.
- *Let other participants respond first* to give you time to gather your thoughts. We use this strategy often because it gives us time to pull ourselves together. It also allows you to facilitate the conversation between participants rather than between you and the participant who made the comment; this puts you in control of the dialogue. When participants are engaging with one another, you can always add to their points to bring more clarity.

Some of the strategies mentioned earlier will work in this situation but here are a few more you might want to try.

- *What do others think about _____?*

- *What's going on for people in the room? I'm noticing a shift in mood.*

- *I'm not sure why, but I'm having an emotional reaction to what was said; is anyone else experiencing some discomfort?* Kathy Obear refers to this as testing for similar reactions. This is where you use what you are experiencing as an indicator. You name what you are feeling, and ask others if they are feeling the same way.

While anger is a healthy and necessary emotion, particularly when it comes to issues related to racism, it is not helpful for the facilitator to lose control and bring it into the workshop environment. When they are able to empathize with participants who have not grown in their understanding of racism, power, and oppression, and at the same time connect to the urgency of eradicating –isms, they are more prepared to bridge the racial divide. Our personal work processing pain and anger should happen outside of the workshop so we are better equipped to cultivate change in others.

## WHEN PARTICIPANTS STOMP ON EACH OTHER'S HEADS

One reason for increasing our cultural competence individually and as a society is to better understand ways we unconsciously harm one another. It's also about taking action to change systems and ourselves so we can develop healthy relationships with our fellow human beings in ways that don't oppress or hurt one another. As the saying goes, "When I knew better, I did better." Far too often we see advocates for social justice engage in the "Oppression Olympics," trying to one-up each other on which group experiences the worst oppression. We also see people trying to shame others into understanding -isms, wanting them to feel bad about their own privileges or the history of oppression. Neither of these approaches is helpful in building relationships for a socially just society or moving people forward in their personal understanding. It is important we engage in conversation in ways that promote growth and a love for justice and each other.

When this happens, take a moment to converse about why this work is important. Reconnect people to each other's humanity.

- *What do you notice happening right now?*
- *How are we working together in this moment? Remember, it is good to feel discomfort, and guilt is a normal feeling associated with this work, but it's not our goal to make each other feel bad. This is about each of us learning and growing in our experience together.*

- *How would you describe how people are treating each other?*
- *Whose interests are being served?*
- *What could we be doing differently to show we are working together to deepen understanding and promote growth?*
- *Let's revisit the purpose of this session. We're all here because we want to see a more socially just society, right? What could we be doing differently?*

## WHEN PARTICIPANTS OF COLOR SAY THEY DON'T THINK THESE CONVERSATIONS ARE NECESSARY

When a person of color says they don't think this workshop is necessary because they haven't experienced racism, or that things are better than they have ever been, it puts you in a difficult position. This is particularly true when there are few participants of color in the room. It could be you were secretly counting on them to help move the conversation forward. This may confirm for your resistant white participants that race isn't an issue any more because "Andrea doesn't think it's a problem, and she's Latina." Below are suggestions for how you might address the person of color's comment.

- Take it from an individual experience to a group experience: *It's good to know that you're not experiencing the pain and frustration associated with racism and discrimination in your personal or professional life. I don't hear that very often from people of color, and I truly wish more could say the same. While your individual experiences are important, we are talking about the overall group experiences of people of color.*
- *While individual experiences are an important part of helping us to understand how racism manifests itself, our conversation today is based on the research of the group's experience.*
- *What has been your experience?* Let them share. *Do you feel the same could be said for the majority of people of color?*
- Ask the group: *Does a person of color experience racism because they are not trying hard enough, don't have the right attitude, or maybe is just being too sensitive?*
- Ask the group: *What factors are often involved when someone experiences racism?* Common reasons: Where they live, go to school, the more they identify with their culture, the darker their skin, the taller or larger they are, being one of few people of color at work, and so on.
- *What are other peoples thoughts about what Andrea just shared?*
- This comment can be made by people of color for different reasons. As hard as this might be to hear, and while we would never say it to participants directly, this comment is evidence to us they are likely operating in denial. Atkinson, Morten, and Sue (1979, 1989, 1998) proposed a five-stage Minority Identity Development model (MID); the first stage is the Conformity Stage, where people of color have "unequivocal preference for dominant cultural values over their own" (296). Sue and Sue (2013) say, "The conformity stage represents, perhaps, the most damning indictment of white racism" (96–97).

People of color who are in this early stage of conformity have reframed their negative experiences, taking the focus off race and redirecting it to the individual's mood, a misunderstanding, and similar things. For example, rather than entertaining the idea that someone ignored them in line to assist a white person, even though they were first, they might say to themselves, "They just didn't see me." Or, if treated poorly, they might think, "The person is just having a bad day." While this may be true, the person of color completely overlooks that race could have been a factor.

Being in the Conformity Stage does not make you immune to the impact of racism. When people start to move further along in their racial/ethnic identity development, they frequently go through a period of intense anger as they come to realize they have assimilated to dominant culture's norms, beliefs, and behaviors as a way to fit in. In essence, they give up who they are, lacking a sense of pride in their own culture. Some would argue that it's better to assimilate. We believe that it's better to be true to yourself.

The following are a few reasons why a person of color might be in denial:

- In an early stage of their identity development.
- Has not yet consciously explored racial experiences.
- Grew up in predominantly white communities and coped by not seeing race.
- Raised outside the United States during formative years.
- Sees racism in the old-fashioned way (e.g., Ku Klux Klan) rather than the more subtle, covert forms.
- Adopted and raised by a white family who minimizes race.
- Unaware of how institutional racism is manifested.

## NAME AND TALK ABOUT NONVERBAL COMMUNICATION HAPPENING IN THE ROOM

When you observe participants communicating nonverbally that they disagree with something said in the room, talk about it. These are opportunities to bring underlying attitudes and thoughts to the surface so courageous conversations can happen.

- *I noticed you sigh when Glen talked about not having any privilege. Can you tell us about what's going on for you?*
- *I noticed the two of you immediately turn and talk to each other after Leslie commented. Did you have a reaction to something she said?*
- *What was going on in your head that caused you to laugh when Diane said _____?*

## ENGAGING THE RESISTANCE (ADAPTED FROM KATHY OBEAR)

When participants show resistance to broadening their lens, avoid getting into a power struggle. You can do this by asking for more information to deepen your knowledge of where they are coming from. The better you understand their thinking, the better your questioning will become. Not only is this approach more likely to shift their thinking, it can also help them dig deeper into the root of their thinking. The key is to become skilled at asking questions. Do this with genuine curiosity and believe what they disclose is true from their perspective. The following are some examples of questions you might ask to gain greater insight into their thinking:

- **Ask for specific examples to illustrate their views.**
  - *I would like to better understand your perspective. Would you give me an example of when your whiteness worked against you?*

- *Help me to better understand why you feel that way. Can you be more specific about how you came to believe _____?*

- *It would help if you could share an example of _____.*

- **Ask for more information to understand their internal frame of reference.**

  - *Tell me more about_____.*

  - *You said_____. Can you expand on that more?*

- **Other strategies**

  - Ask for clarification.

  - Paraphrase to check for accuracy.

  - Reflect their feelings: *I may be totally off, but I'm sensing that you are frustrated. What's going on for you right now?*

  - Ask another participant to share their understanding of what is being said.


## DON'T RESCUE WHITE PEOPLE FROM THEIR DISCOMFORT

It is common in conversations about racism for white people to become emotional or defensive as they come to terms with their privilege and the impact of racism. Many well-meaning people, including facilitators, may want to comfort them in a difficult moment. It's important we allow whites to wrestle with their dis-ease so they can work through feelings of guilt or blame. Reassuring someone that it's "okay" or they are "still a good person" robs them of the opportunity to go deeper. Here are suggestions for what you can do as a facilitator to encourage deeper reflection:

- *What do you hear Ray saying? How is this different from the way you thought or wanted to believe things were?*
- *What are you feeling right now? Talk to us about why you are crying.*
- *What's going on for you?*
- *It seems like this activity really impacted you. Would you like to talk about it?*
- *I can see this is difficult for you to hear. I encourage you to stay with the discomfort and talk about it.*
- *It's easy to move to an intellectual place. You seem to be feeling a lot of emotions. Stay with your feelings, and see if you can get in touch with them and process out loud what's going on for you.*
- *What you are experiencing as a result of this activity is a common experience that people of color have. I appreciate you engaging, despite how difficult it is. When people are silent about racism, it's often at the expense of people of color.*
- *How has what your peers shared influenced your perspective?*


## DON'T DO ALL THE WORK

When you find yourself trying to "convince" participants that what you are saying is true, STOP!!!! You're working too hard. You will frequently come across resistant participants whom you struggle with. It's easy to get caught in a trap of trying to "persuade" them to see things the way you do. For example, when talking about racism you might say:

> *People of color are still finding it difficult to get promoted or hired into management positions. If you look at the structure of many organizations, you will still find in the 21st century whites in management positions and people of color in lower-level staff or entry-level positions.* A white resistant participant might respond by saying, *I was actually told by someone at one organization not to apply for a management position because they wanted to hire a person of color. Now people of color are getting jobs that whites can't get because the jobs are being saved for them. No one is talking about reverse discrimination.*

This is often the moment when tension heightens in the room. You may be the first to try to explain the differences, but before you finish, several hands go up. Participants of color and sometimes white allies will try to explain how their example is different from racism. Participants of color will start to share their experiences of racism only to be told by the resistant participant that they had that same experience, with statements like this: "I was followed in the store too." They will totally miss the point you and others are referring to an ongoing collective experience of racism, versus an individual experience of bias or prejudice that occurs one or two times in a lifetime.

The more resistance that occurs, the more attempts people might make to cite research, define equity, give examples, and explain the differences. There will be some participants in the room who think the same way as the resistant participant, but who will remain silent because they do not want to be put in the hot seat. The conversation is getting nowhere. You are frustrated because you can't seem to penetrate the resistant participant's thinking, and maybe you start to question your own skills and abilities. Participants of color are frustrated because they have shared very personal and painful experiences of racism, which are being relived in that moment to no avail, and the resistant participant is frustrated because she is likely feeling attacked. All in all, emotions are high.

This is the moment when you realize things are getting out of control. When this happens, step in and interrupt the process. No one is listening to anyone because everyone is planted firmly in their belief systems. It has now become a power struggle of who is right and who is wrong. The resistant person becomes the "bad" object who just doesn't get it, furthering the racial divide, creating an "us against you" type mentality. The best thing you can do in these situations is to end the conversation and name what you see happening in the room. Thank participants for speaking their truth and taking risks, including the resistant participant whose voice represents the view of many people in and outside of the room. No amount of research or personal examples are going to permeate that person's thinking. They have put up walls that you are not going to knock down. Remind yourself you have planted seeds for another time in their life when someone invites them to engage in race conversations. Here's an example of what you might say:

> *We could spend a lot more time on this conversation, but I'm concerned where this is going. I feel like everyone is trying to convince Emily that racism still exists, and I'm worried that participants are having to give too much of themselves in order to prove that it's real and different from individual experiences of bias. I'm also worried about Emily. She has been alone at the center of this conversation for a while representing a voice that is not just her beliefs but the beliefs of many people. So I'm going to stop us from continuing on further because I think it will only divide us more rather than bring us closer together in understanding. I hope that some of our white allies in*

*the room will take the time to engage Emily during a break or at some other time, if you (looking at Emily) are interested. I want to thank you, Emily, for taking risk and speaking your truth. I imagine it wasn't easy. Thank you for staying in the conversation with us. We can't have courageous conversations if people keep their thoughts and beliefs to themselves. I also want to thank participants who gave of themselves once again to help Emily explore other ways of thinking about racism. It is painful to retell experiences of racism, and it often comes at a huge price. So thank you for your vulnerability and commitment to social justice. This is hard work for everyone involved, and the costs are high. This is one of those times when we will need to expect and accept nonclosure.*

While things did not go as you hoped, an approach like this does keep the conversation from spiraling too far out of control. Some of what happens in the room will be helpful, even if you are unable to see the fruits of your labor. And some of what happened could have been avoided. In either case, there are never any clear-cut answers for how to navigate these waters.

## STOP AND REFLECT

What are some ways that you could respond to this comment, "Talking about race divides us rather than brings us together. We should focus on what we have in common, not our differences"? What questions might you ask?

_____

_____

_____

_____

_____

_____

_____

_____

_____

_____

_____

_____

_____

# Chapter Thirty

## Balancing Humor and the Seriousness of the Issue

A little kingdom I possess, where thoughts and feelings dwell; And very hard the task I find of governing it well.

—Louisa May Alcott

Having conversations about race is anxiety-provoking and can bring up an array of emotions. Laughter can be helpful in dealing with the unease. For many it serves as a way to cope with experiences of oppression, make fun of our own humanness when we make mistakes, or it can be a way to relieve anxiety and tension in the room. It's important in these conversations that we take time out to laugh with one another and at ourselves. At the same time, we have to be cautious that our laughter does not occur at critical moments that may cause people to feel unheard or dismissed. Sometimes humor can backfire if it is at the expense of others or if it triggers a bad experience they've had.

- *Laughing eases the anxiety*

   Sometimes laughing can help to ease the anxiety and can also convey a message that we all make mistakes when it comes to race relations. After you have laughed together, take a moment to explain the gifts that laughing brings, and the dangers it can pose.

   Research shows that sharing laughter creates a bond between people. It builds our relationships and trust of one another.

   If you can use laughter early in the workshop, participants will feel more connected and open to what you have to share.

- *Using humor at the wrong time*

   Be careful not to use humor at the wrong times. Sitting in the tension can be a good thing that promotes growth, allowing participants to experience discomfort and deal with serious issues.

   I've used humor to lighten the mood in a workshop, just as someone was starting to explore his own internalized stereotypes. This came from my own discomfort and prevented him from going deeper into some of the hurt and the healing.

135

• *When using humor offends*

*My apologies for joking around about something so serious. I could see that you were not smiling. I'm realizing that it was probably something that was hurtful to you. Would you like to talk about it?*

*Thank you, Latisha, for sharing your discomfort with the fact that we all laughed at what was said. While humor can be good sometimes, it can also be at the expense of another person's pain.*

*Thank you, Devon. I appreciate your taking a risk and sharing how angry it made you feel to hear us all laughing. I want to apologize, because as a leader of this workshop, when I laugh, I'm giving other people permission to do the same.*

*I noticed that not everyone was laughing. Would anyone who didn't laugh be willing to share what was going on for you when we were laughing?*

Humor is perhaps a sense of intellectual perspective: an awareness that some things are really important, others not; and that the two kinds are most oddly jumbled in everyday affairs.

—Christopher Morley

# Chapter Thirty-One

## Role-Playing Activity

To make the structure of a difficult conversation visible, we need to understand not only what is said, but also what is not said. We need to understand what the people involved are thinking and feeling but not saying to each other. In a difficult conversation, this is usually where the real action is.

—Douglas Stone, Bruce Patton, and Sheila Heen

**Norm:** *Experience Discomfort*

**W**hen learning a new skill, particularly for situations that provoke anxiety in us, it's important that we practice again and again. That way, the desired new response becomes our immediate reaction when the challenging situation occurs. You will only remember 10 percent of what you read but 90 percent of what you do and say.

## INSTRUCTIONS

Total Activity Time: (approximately 45 minutes)

This activity can be done in dyads, triads, or small groups of 4 or 5 participants. The following are suggested instructions for how to do this activity with 4 or 5 people. Modify if you have fewer, omitting the timekeeper and observer if necessary. There are 5 vignettes to choose from to role-play.

1. **Choose Roles** (2 min)

    Decide who will be the facilitator, the workshop participant, the observer, and the timekeeper. See below for description of roles. It's important that you choose roles before reading and discussing the vignette so you can read closely with that role in mind.

2. **Choose and Read Vignette** (3 minutes)

3. **Group Discussion** (10 minutes)

    Discuss group questions at the bottom of the vignette. Before role-playing, help prepare the person who will be role-playing the facilitator by coming up with ideas for how they might respond during the role-play.

4. **Role-Play** (5 minutes)
   Role-play vignette. Try to make this as real as possible.

5. **Processing by Facilitator and Participant** (15 minutes)
   Once you are finished role-playing, take time to process. This is an opportunity for the facilitator and participant to process their experiences. Everyone else will listen while they process. Do not interrupt, explain, or add any comments. Additional participants do not process during this time.

6. **Note Taker/Observer** (5 min)
   Give feedback, building on what participants noticed about themselves and add things they may not have been aware of.

7. **Cross-Group Dialogue** (5 minutes)
   This is an opportunity for anyone to say or respond to anything that has been said or occurred during the processing portion of this activity.

8. **Reverse Roles and Repeat Process**
   If there is time, assign new roles and try it again. You can either choose another vignette or practice the same one again. Sometimes it's helpful to try the same one now that you have had a chance to discuss successes and challenges.


## ROLES

1. **Note Taker/Observer**
   Take notes only during the role-playing portion of this activity. Your role is to take notes and give feedback to the participant and facilitator on their body language, the way things were worded, reactions, visible discomfort, where they appeared to struggle, and what they did well. Think of what questions you might ask to help process. When you are done, comment on how it felt to give feedback to the participant and facilitator.
   **Note**: *It is difficult giving people constructive feedback, and will be a skill you need for facilitating conversations on race and other -isms. Think of this as an opportunity to practice.*

**Examples:**

- (To the facilitator) *I noticed that you seemed to be very nervous at first, and you confirmed it when you were processing. You stuttered a lot and said "um" frequently. But after about 3 minutes into it, you appeared to loosen up. Do you tend to be nervous when presenting or talking to a group, or is it this particular role-playing situation that created the anxiety?*
- (To the participant) *At what point did you feel yourself begin to let down your defenses?*
- (To the participant) *When the facilitator said, "_____," what reaction did you have? I'm curious to know if her comment made you shut down more or did it cause you to want to engage.*

2. **Participant** (You may need to play a race or gender different from your own. Avoid stereotyping in your portrayal.)

In your role as a participant try to realistically act out how you imagine that person being. Don't make it too simple for the facilitator, but don't make it unrealistically difficulty either. This means that you will have to pay attention to not only what the facilitator does or says but also how it makes you feel. Respond based on the impact their words and actions have on you.

When processing, discuss how you felt. Was anything said that you internally responded positively to? Was anything said that you had a negative reaction to? Think about verbal and nonverbal communication.

**Note:** *This role will help you to imagine what might be going on for the resistant participant and can offer insight into what works and what doesn't. Empathy and knowledge are keys to your success.*

3. **Facilitator** (Do not change your race or gender to role-play.)

Role-playing the facilitator is the hardest role because you are trying something new, and all eyes are on you. However, it's the best role to have because you have the unique opportunity to practice new strategies. Relax and have fun with it. Don't try to be perfect in it. Instead, play with your role as a facilitator and try different things. See what reactions you get from the participant when you say or do certain things. What you learn from this experience will help you become a more skilled facilitator when faced with a real-life situation.

When processing, discuss how you feel about how you did in your role. Was there anything the participants said that you had an emotional response to? What would you have done or said differently? What did you say that felt right?

**Note:** *This will help you to practice your role as a facilitator. We are constantly practicing who we want to become.*

4. **Timekeeper**

The timekeeper is very important. Practice using skills of interrupting and warning when there is 1 minute left and stopping the conversations when it is time.

**Note:** *Managing time, interrupting, and ending are all necessary parts of effective facilitation. If you are not used to interrupting, this will be good practice for you.*

5. **Additional Participants/Observers**

You have two roles. First, you will be an additional participant or member of the audience. You can participate when you are prompted to by the facilitator or when it feels natural to jump in to help with the role-play. Your participation can be verbal or nonverbal. You will decide how to best fit in. Your involvement should enhance the role-playing process. Read the role of the facilitator and participant so that you are clear on what they are being asked to do.

Your second role is to be an observer. Provide input during the Cross-Group Dialogue portion of this activity. You do not partake when the facilitator and participant process.

**Note:** *Jumping in at any given moment is something that facilitators have to do often. Practicing this skill will help you become more comfortable with risk-taking. Also, providing critical feedback in ways that help people grow will be necessary.*

**Examples of Feedback during Cross-Group Dialogue**

- *Michael* (participant) *said he shut down when you* (facilitator) *said "_____." Did you pick up on his change in behavior when you made that comment, and also, what would you try differently if given another chance?*
- *Michael, was there something in particular about her comment that caused you to shut down? What could she have said that would have kept you receptive to engaging?*


## VIGNETTES

The following vignettes come from real workshops and commonly recur. Use the role-play guidelines to practice responding so you will be ready to facilitate these situations.


### #1 White Male Privilege

You are a staff member and in charge of facilitating a workshop that is mandatory for all staff. Because of the size of the organization, some of the staff know one another, and others do not. You yourself do not know everyone. The group is fairly diverse but predominantly white. A white male comes in and sits outside of the group in the far back corner of the room. You invite him to join one of the table groups, and he says, with disinterest, "I'm fine where I am."

You proceed to facilitate the workshop. You notice that his arms are crossed and his head is down, as if he is trying to sleep. Fifteen minutes later you start the first group activity, which involves table discussions. He is still sitting alone with the same body language.

### Questions to Explore

1. What is he messaging to you through his body language and actions?
2. What is he likely feeling or thinking?
3. How are you feeling? Where are those feelings coming from?
4. How might you respond?
5. What are some things that you need to avoid doing or saying?
6. Explore how the facilitator might utilize their gender or race in this situation. For example, if the facilitator is a white male, is there something he might say to connect to this participant? Or, how might a Native American female facilitator engage, given their differences? Explore other racial and gender dynamics.


### #2 Racism and Classism

You are facilitating a workshop on white privilege using Peggy McIntosh's work *White Privilege & Male Privilege: A Personal Account of Coming to See Correspondences through Work in Women Studies.* Ongoing workshops are offered throughout the year and employees must choose four to attend. During the discussion period, a young white woman sitting up front becomes somewhat emotional and says, "I grew up poor. We lived in a trailer when I was growing up. I paid my own way through college while raising my two children as a single parent. I don't feel privileged, and I don't like the fact that you are saying that my life was easier because I'm white. I worked hard to get where I am, and if others do the same, they can better their lives too."

## Questions to Explore

1. Who is she referring to when saying "others"?
2. What is she likely feeling?
3. How are you feeling? Where are those feelings coming from?
4. How might you respond?
5. What are some things you need to avoid doing or saying?
6. Explore how the facilitator might utilize their gender or race in this situation. For example, if the facilitator is a white woman, is there something she might say to connect to this participant? Or, how might an African-American female facilitator engage given their differences and similarities? Explore other racial and gender dynamics.

### #3 Blaming the Victim

You are facilitating an optional workshop that participants signed up for to learn new skills and strategies to address racism in the workplace. Of the 25 participants, 4 are people of color.

During introductions, a white woman says, "I really hope we're going to spend some time today talking about the victim mentality that so many people of color have. Many of our problems with race wouldn't exist if they didn't create the barriers to our relationships or if they actually believed that they could succeed and it wasn't 'acting white' to work hard."

## Questions to Explore

1. What do you think she means when she says, "victim mentality"?
2. Why might she feel so strongly about this? What do you think might be going on for her?
3. How are you feeling? Where are those feelings coming from?
4. How might you respond?
5. What are some things that you need to avoid doing or saying?
6. Explore how the facilitator might utilize their gender or race in this situation. For example, if the facilitator is a white woman, is there something she might say to connect to this participant? Or, how might an Asian male facilitator engage given their differences? Explore other racial and gender dynamics.

### #4 Assimilation

You are facilitating the first mandatory full-day workshop on institutional racism for a group of 40 people who all work for the same organization. Everyone knows everyone. About two hours into the workshop, you mention that many people of color feel as though they have to leave a part of themselves behind when they go into the workplace.

A Mexican American man says, "I don't have to give up any part of myself in order to go to work. I treat people with basic respect—how I want to be treated. Besides, we're all just here to get our jobs done, not to have some kind of touchy feely love-fest."

**Questions to Explore**

1. What is he saying about cultural competence work, and why might he be saying this?
2. How are you feeling? Where are those feelings coming from?
3. How might you respond?
4. What are some things that you need to avoid doing or saying?
5. Explore how the facilitator might utilize their gender or race in this situation. For example, if the facilitator is a Latino male, is there something he might say to connect to this participant? Or, how might a white female facilitator engage given their differences? Explore other racial and gender dynamics.

## #5 Color-Blind

You are hired to facilitate a workshop titled "What Is Cultural Competence?" for an elementary school where the demographics are rapidly changing from primarily all white students to majority students from diverse racial, ethnic, and religious backgrounds. Most of the certified teachers attend, but only 1 or 2 classified staff are present because of lack of funding. Ninety-five percent of your audience is white, and a number of them have been teaching at this school for many years. You introduce yourself, go over the goals for the day, and review the norms. So far everything has gone smoothly. You receive positive affirmation from some of your audience members through their body language. However, you also notice that there are far too many participants who appear unresponsive. Only a few are laughing at your jokes, and, overall, people seem tense. This is increasing your anxiety.

You move into the warm-up activity to get them engaged and then have them brainstorm out loud while you record on flip chart paper their responses to the question, "What does being Culturally Competent mean to you?" Participants give great responses, and things seem to be picking up. You do a nice job of giving them positive feedback and affirming their definition. But then a white woman participant says in a somewhat defensive tone, "It sounds like you are saying we need to know about every culture we work with. I have been teaching in this district for over 25 years, and I treat all of my students the same. I don't care if they are brown, blue, yellow, or purple!"

**Questions to Explore**

1. What might being going on for her and why?
2. How are you feeling? Where are those feelings coming from?
3. How might you respond?
4. What are some things that you need to avoid doing or saying?
5. Explore how the facilitator might utilize their gender or race in this situation. For example, if the facilitator is a Filipino woman, is there something she might say to connect to this participant? Or, how might an African-American male facilitator engage given their differences? Explore other racial and gender dynamics. How might your experience with the education system tie in?

# SECTION VI
# APPENDICES

# Appendix A

## This Is the Hour

The Hopi Nation Elders of Oraibi, Arizona

You have been telling the people that this is the Eleventh Hour.
Now you must go back and tell the people that this is the Hour.
And there are things to be considered:
Where are you living?
What are you doing?
What are your relationships?
Are you in right relation?
Where is your water?
Know your garden.
It is time to speak your Truth.
Create your community.
Be good to each other.
And do not look outside yourself for the leader.
This could be a good time!
There is a river flowing now very fast.
It is so great and swift that there are those who will be afraid.
They will try to hold onto the shore.
They will feel they are being torn apart and they will suffer greatly.
Know the river has its destination.
The elders say we must let go of the shore, push off into the middle of the river, keep our eyes open
    and our heads above the water.
See who is in there with you and celebrate.
At this time in history, we are to take nothing personally.
Least of all, ourselves.
For the moment that we do, our spiritual growth and journey comes to a halt.
The time of the lone wolf is over.
Gather yourselves!
Banish the word struggle from your attitude and your vocabulary.
All that we do now must be done in a sacred manner and in celebration.
We are the ones we've been waiting for.

# Appendix B

## Checklist of What to Bring

**D**o you have everything you need? It's helpful to be as organized as possible. A checklist of what to bring can help you stay on top of things. There is nothing worse than arriving at your workshop and realizing you forgot something important. We keep a checklist of what to bring at the bottom of our agenda and check each item off once it is packed in the bag. Many of these things can or will be provided by the organization. The following are some examples of what you might need for your workshop:

__ 3 x 5 cards
__ Baskets for table supplies
__ Blank paper
__ Business cards
__ Certificates of participation
__ Colored pencils or crayons
__ Computer
__ Easel
__ Evaluations
__ Extra pens and pencils
__ Fliers for upcoming events
__ Flip-chart paper
__ Food/Treats/Coffee/Tea
__ Handouts
__ Highlighters
__ Laptop

__ Markers
__ Music
__ Name tags
__ Norm cards
__ Painters tape
__ Poem for closing
__ Posters on wall
__ Posters or PowerPoint with quotes
__ PowerPoint clicker
__ Projector
__ Resource books
__ Sign-in sheet
__ Speakers
__ Tablecloth for resources
__ USB drive
__ Your agenda

# Appendix C

## Norms

Norms for engaging in conversations about racism and privilege are not the same norms used when you are meeting to discuss budget or other general organizational issues. When setting up the norms for any meeting you are informing participants of what is to be expected, in some cases, what are "normal" experiences they are likely to have during your workshop. Norms are helpful for setting the tone and letting participants know what to expect in themselves and of one another. These norms are designed to intentionally counter some of the norms of dominant white culture. You may want to explain that when norms are not explicitly talked about, they favor those who are best versed in the dominant culture.

You will find yourself relying heavily on your norms as participants move deeper into conversations about race. Therefore, it's important you take time, at least 10 to 15 minutes, to review them at the beginning of your workshop. Post them on table tents or poster paper. They should only have the norms themselves on them and not the explanations. Explaining their meaning is your work. Be sure to think about examples that you can share that bring understanding of how these norms are used. The following is a list of norms and examples of what we often say about them to help develop understanding. These norms were adapted from the work of Glenn Singleton.

### STAY ENGAGED

- It's important that you try to stay present in the room. Pay attention to when you are shutting down. Discomfort and anxiety are normal parts of courageous conversations.
- If you find yourself needing to stand up, please do so. It's a long day, and we have a lot of hard work to do. If you find yourself drifting, use strategies that will help you stay present.
- Stay with the topic. When you feel discomfort it's easy to take the conversation some place different. Resist the urge to change the topic to another -ism. One reason it's hard to stay on the topic of racism is that it can bring up issues of guilt, shame, and anger. However difficult it may become, we want you to stay engaged in this race conversation.
- Checking out of the conversation when it becomes uncomfortable is one form of privilege protection.

## SPEAK YOUR TRUTH

- The purpose of having these conversations is to be able to speak our truths about our ex periences. If not here, where? If not now, when?
- We often avoid speaking our truth for fear of what others might say. It's important that we create an environment where everyone is free to speak openly so that learning can occur.
- People are in different places in this work. In order for us to grow, it's important people are able to share their thoughts in a way that's comfortable for them.
- When we share our thoughts, it often creates an emotional reaction from others. Being able to speak your truth does not mean that people will not respond emotionally. Be prepared to experience the discomfort that race conversations bring.
- Speaking our truth does not mean stomping on each other's heads. Before speaking, think about what it is that you want others to know. How can they best hear you? Whose interests are being served? When speaking, are you creating enemies or allies? When you speak, are you speaking to put others down or put them in their place, or are you speaking so that new learning can occur for others in the room?
- Remember that everyone does not communicate in the same way you do. If someone gets loud in the room, it doesn't mean they are angry. If they are angry, it doesn't necessarily mean they are angry with you. If they are angry with something you said, it doesn't mean that person no longer has a relationship with you. Oftentimes these conversations bring up a lot of emotions from past and present experiences. Allow others to experience their emotions without your shutting down.
- One of the characteristics of dominance is to speak as if you represent all people's perspectives rather than just your own. We call this the "universal you," as in, "You know how we enjoy chocolate?" The universal you also allows you to say something without taking personal ownership of your opinions. Try to avoid the universal you and instead speak for yourself by making "I" instead of "We" statements.

## NO FIXING

- It is human nature to want to fix other people's pain and discomfort, particularly when they are crying or clearly distressed. However, it's important that we let each person in the room experience their own discomfort and not fix it for them. This is a part of their learning.
- Sometimes people will want to "fix" each other by reassuring them about their lack of stereotypes or racism. This is often the case when they share that identity with the person who is acknowledging their biases. For example, a white woman telling another white woman she's not prejudiced. If you find yourself wanting to fix someone, explore what might be coming up about your own identity.
- If you find yourself wanting to "fix" a situation or make someone feel better, pause for a moment and reflect on what is going on in you.

## EXPERIENCE DISCOMFORT

- One way to think about this is: "Learn to become comfortable with the discomfort." In other words, being uncomfortable is to be expected.
- If you are not feeling any sense of discomfort in the dialogue, ask yourself if you are fully engaged? Are you giving of yourself fully and taking risks?
- Many people confuse safety and comfort. You can have perfectly safe conversations where people are very uncomfortable.
- Often, people who are experiencing oppression will be blamed for making members of the dominant culture uncomfortable. You may hear, "Race wasn't an issue before these workshops created all the problems." Avoiding conversations for the sake of comfort serves to reinforce white privilege.

## TAKE RISKS

- The more you are willing to risk, the more potential you have to learn.
- By staying silent out of the fear of saying something wrong, avoiding conflict, or making someone else uncomfortable, you miss the opportunity to authentically engage with one another. You also miss out on the opportunity to grow in your understanding.

## LISTEN FOR UNDERSTANDING

- Try to understand where another person is coming from as best you can.
- Be careful not to compare your experiences with another person's. For example, saying gender oppression is the same as racial oppression. This often invalidates or minimizes a person's experiences.
- Listen without thinking about how you are going to respond.
- Stay present in their pain and your discomfort as you listen.
- If someone is pointing out how what you said left them feeling, try not to explain or rationalize what you said or why you said it. For example, sometimes it's necessary to just say, "I didn't realize what I said was inappropriate," or "I didn't mean to hurt you. I'm sorry."
- Think about your comments before saying them. Resist the need to explain. Sometimes positive intent is not enough (intent vs. impact). Be careful not to lose the opportunity to just listen. Don't put the focus back on you.

## EXPECT AND ACCEPT NONCLOSURE

- In our society today, we often want to feel some sense of closure, regardless of the issue. There will be fortunate situations where you will be able to resolve something between you and another person, but more often it will feel unfinished. Sometimes you will have to circle back around at another time to reconcile differences and other times you will have to sit with nonclosure.
- Engaging in race conversations means there will be times of no closure. This is ongoing work that does not necessarily leave one walking away feeling like everything turned out

the way you hoped. Be willing to take risks, and accept that much of this is about changing yourself, not others.

- White cultural norms focus on the product, rather than the process. These are process conversations where greater awareness leads to future changes.

**Note**: When we explain the norms, we do not open up an opportunity for participants to provide suggestions for what norms they believe we should hold in the room. We take the lead as facilitators by naming these norms for them. When you allow participants to provide their own thinking around norms, you run the risk of having to tell them early on in the day that what they think doesn't apply in this situation. We will answer questions and clarify the norms for participants.

Adapted from Singleton and Linton (2006).

# Appendix D

## What Is Cultural Competence?

**A** culturally competent professional is one who is actively in the process of becoming aware of his or her own assumptions about human behavior, values, biases, preconceived notions, personal limitations, and so forth.

Second, a culturally competent professional is one who actively attempts to understand the worldview of culturally diverse populations. In other words, what are the values, assumptions, practices, communication styles, group norms, biases, experiences, perspectives and so on, of culturally diverse students, families, communities and colleagues you interact with?

Third, a culturally competent professional is one who is in the process of actively developing and practicing appropriate, relevant, and sensitive strategies and skills in working with culturally diverse students, families, communities, and colleagues.

Fourth, a culturally competent professional is one who advocates on behalf of the needs of their students, clients, families, colleagues they work with. They take action in their work place, community and society to create a culture of respect and equity.

Thus, cultural competence is an active, developmental, ongoing process and is aspirational rather than achieved.

### CULTURAL COMPETENCE: AWARENESS

1. *The culturally competent professional is one who has moved from being culturally unaware to being aware and sensitive to their own cultural heritage and to valuing and respecting differences.*

   - The professional has begun the process of exploring their values, standards, and assumptions about human behavior.

   - Rather than being ethnocentric and believing in the superiority of their group's cultural heritage (arts, traditions, language, etc.), there is acceptance and respect for cultural differences.

   - Other cultural and sociodemographic groups are seen as equally valuable and legitimate.

   - The professional has knowledge of their own heritage including history, traditions, culture, and assimilation into dominant culture.

2. *The culturally competent professional is aware of his or her own values, beliefs, and biases and how they may affect members of oppressed groups.*

   - The professional actively and constantly attempts to avoid prejudices, unwarranted labeling, and stereotyping (e.g., African Americans and Latin@ Americans are intellectually inferior and will not do well in school, Asian Americans make good technical workers but poor managers, women belong in the home, people with physical disabilities can't lead productive lives, or the elderly are no longer useful in society).

   - Culturally competent professionals do not hold preconceived limitations and notions about culturally diverse people.

   - The professional actively challenges his or her assumptions, tries to find effective ways to work cross-culturally, and seeks consultation, supervision, and culturally relevant professional development.

3. *Culturally competent professionals are comfortable with differences that exist between themselves and others in terms of race, gender, sexual orientation, and other sociodemographic variables. Differences are not seen as negative.*

   - The culturally competent professional does not profess colorblindness or negate the existence of differences in behavior, attitudes, cultural norms, beliefs, and so on among different groups.

4. *The culturally competent professional is sensitive to circumstances (personal biases; stage of racial, gender, and sexual orientation identity development; sociopolitical influences, etc.) that may dictate referral of a student, client, or staff to a member of their own sociodemographic group or to another professional in general.*

   - A culturally competent professional is aware of their limitations and is not threatened by the prospect of seeking assistance and support from others. However, …

   - This principle should not be used as a cop-out for the professional who does not want to work with culturally diverse students, clients, or staff, or who do not want to work through their own personal biases.

5. *The culturally competent professional acknowledges and is aware of their own racist, sexist, heterosexist, or other detrimental attitudes, beliefs, behaviors, and feelings.*

   - A culturally competent professional does not deny the fact that they have directly or indirectly benefited from individual, institutional, and cultural biases and that they have been socialized into such a society. As a result, the culturally competent professional inherits elements in the socialization process that may be detrimental to people of color and other marginalized groups.

   - Culturally competent professionals accept responsibility for their own racism, sexism, heterosexism, and so on, and attempt to deal with them in a nondefensive, guilt-free manner. They have begun the process of defining a new nonoppressive and nonexploitive attitude. In terms of racism, for example, addressing one's whiteness (e.g., white privilege) is crucial.

## CULTURAL COMPETENCE: KNOWLEDGE

1. *The culturally competent professional must possess specific knowledge and information about the particular groups they are working with.*

   - The professional must be aware of the history, experiences, cultural values, and lifestyles of various sociodemographic groups in our society.

   - The professional understands the idea that the greater the depth of knowledge of one cultural group and the more knowledge the professional has of many groups, the more likely it is that they can be effective in their role.

   - Thus, the culturally competent professional is one who continues to explore and learn about different cultures and the many problems marginalized groups encounter, throughout their professional career.

2. *The culturally competent professional will have a good understanding of the sociopolitical systems operating in the United States with respect to treatment of marginalized groups.*

   - The culturally competent professional understands the impact and operation of oppression (racism, sexism, heterosexism, etc.), the politics of systemic privilege, and the racist, sexist, and homophobic concepts that have permeated institutions.

   - Especially valuable is an understanding of the role that ethnocentric monoculturalism plays in the development of identity and worldviews among marginalized groups of people. In other words, people of color may be in a place of seeing their own ethnic or racial group as superior to all others, which is a normal part of identity development.

3. *The culturally competent professional must have clear and explicit knowledge and understanding of the generic characteristics in individuals from diverse ethnic, racial, and socioeconomic backgrounds.*

   - These encompass language factors, culture-bound values, and class-bound values. The professional should understand the value assumptions (normality and abnormality) inherent in systemic oppression.

   - In some cases, applying theories or models to a particular group may limit the potential of persons from different cultures. Likewise, being able to determine those that may be useful to culturally and ethnically diverse individuals is important.

4. *The culturally competent professional is aware of institutional barriers that prevent some people from historically marginalized groups from accessing services.*

   - Important factors include the location of services, the formality or informality of décor, advertising services and events in English only, organizational climate, hours and days of operation, transportation, childcare, and when and how services/events are viewed by some cultures.

## CULTURAL COMPETENCE: SKILLS

1. ***The culturally competent professional must be able to send and receive both verbal and nonverbal messages accurately and appropriately.***
   - The culturally skilled professional must be able not only to communicate (send) their thoughts and feelings, but also to read (receive) both verbal and nonverbal messages.
   - Sending and receiving a message accurately means the ability to consider cultural cues operating within a setting.
   - Accuracy of communication must be tempered by its appropriateness. In many cultures, subtlety and indirectness are appreciated. Likewise, others appreciate directness and confrontation.
   - The culturally skilled professional develops and practices a wide repertoire of responses and pedagogy to effectively work with people from diverse cultures.

2. ***The culturally competent professional is able to exercise a variety of relationship-building skills when working across cultures.***
   - They attend special events, outreach, act as a change agent, and make home/community visits when appropriate.
   - The culturally competent professional actively works to build trust across cultures, particularly where there are systemic barriers or there is a history of oppressive practices.

3. ***The culturally competent professional is aware of their helping style, recognizes limitations that they possess, and can anticipate the impact on culturally diverse students, families, clients, and co-workers.***
   - They acknowledge their limitations and consult with other professionals.
   - They don't do for others what they can do for themselves but rather work with them to find effective solutions. Their approach is supportive instead of paternalistic.
   - They see people they work with as the experts of their own lives as opposed to approaching from a superior attitude: "I know what's best for you."
   - They take into consideration cultural values and norms of the person they are working with rather than trying to force onto them dominant culture ways of doing.
   - They can effectively communicate a desire to help.
   - Culturally competent professionals participate in ongoing, culturally relevant professional development and see themselves as learners.

4. ***The culturally competent professional is able to engage in courageous conversations around the impact of what they said or did that was offensive with the person who was offended.***
   - They have a nondefensive attitude, seeking to learn rather than justify their actions.
   - They actively listen for understanding and ask questions without negating or invalidating the reality of the person they are speaking with.

- Culturally competent professionals accept responsibility for their words or actions and notice when they have a negative impact on others, even if the person affected doesn't bring it up.

- These things may communicate several things to the people you are working with. First, that you are open and honest about your style of communication and the limitations or barriers it may cause; second, that you understand enough about their world-view to anticipate how this may adversely affect them; third, that as a professional, it is important for you to communicate your desire to help despite your limitations; and fourth, that you care enough to do something different.

5. ***The culturally competent professional brings up their own racial difference and the effect of that difference on individual or group dynamics.***

   - They are aware when tension exists in cross-cultural relationships and name the tension.

   - They understand and have open discussions about the historical and current exploitation by people who look like them.

   - They engage in conversation about what is said and what is not said in relation to identity issues.

6. ***The culturally competent professional is skilled at communicating empathy for race-related oppression and marginalization without bringing in their own experiences of different -isms.***

   - They avoid comparisons or the "Oppression Olympics."

   - They believe what they hear without trying to attribute it to experiences or factors they personally are more familiar or comfortable with.

   - Culturally competent professionals ask questions and listen for understanding rather than trying to draw parallels with their own experiences.

   - They understand intersectionality of identities, for example, how race, disability and class are related.

Adapted from Sue and Sue 2003.

## CULTURAL COMPETENCE: ADVOCACY/ACTION

(Adapted from Judith H. Katz)

Cultural Racism:

> These aspects of society that overtly and covertly attribute value and normality to white people and whiteness, and devalue, stereotype, and label people of color as "other", different, less than, or render them invisible.

> —Adams, Bell, and Griffin, *Teaching for Diversity and Social Justice*

1. *The culturally competent professional advocates on behalf of those who are marginalized and takes action within their organization to change institutional policy and practice that benefits some groups at the expense of others. They seek ways to eliminate institutional racism and work to create a welcoming and inclusive culture where everyone benefits. They do this in a way that honors every person's humanity, including those who dispute this change.*

*Ways to combat racism:*

- Educate co-workers and close friends about racism.
- Raise issues in your workplace with people in power, co-workers, and staff.
- Change what normally appears on bulletin boards, walls, handouts, newsletters, and other materials to create an inclusive environment.
- Be a referral resource—direct individuals to people or groups who might be of assistance.
- Act as a role model, take risks, and question the white power structure.
- Establish discussion groups and other activities around race, ethnicity, and culture (e.g., book studies, films, journal articles, exercises, etc.).
- Allocate and use resources in a way that promotes equity for students, staff, and clients of color.
- Assess the cultural environment of your workplace to ensure that it reflects and honors the diversity of students, staff, and clients (e.g., websites, activities/events, décor, the number and positions held by staff of color).
- Seek out and actively participate in culturally relevant professional development (CRPD) aimed to enhance your own awareness, knowledge, and skills in effectively working cross-culturally.
- Contribute time, talent, and treasure to organizations or programs that actively confront oppression.
- Examine policies within your organization to see if they meet the needs of diverse students, staff, and clients.
- Openly disagree with racist comments, jokes, emails, and actions of those around you.
- Take the time to complain to those in charge when you notice racism inside and outside of your work place.
- Demonstrate a willingness to change self versus others as it relates to cultural norms, values, behaviors, and attitudes.
- Develop an "Equity Team" to include people from various levels of the organization to work together to advocate for institutional change.
- Question the norms of meetings to ensure equity.
- Review hiring policy and practices to include diversity beyond legal jargon.
- Move beyond common practice to hire, retain, and promote staff of color to ensure that there is diverse representation.
- Review the mission and vision of your organization to include equity and social justice.
- Make sure that your organization's evaluation and assessment tools take into consideration issues of racism, power, privilege, and oppression.
- Work on political campaigns that increase institutional access for oppressed groups (e.g., immigration laws and marriage equality).
- Screen materials for multicultural content and anti-bias qualities.

- Include diverse ethnic and socioeconomic representation in decision-making, ensuring those most impacted are part of the decision-making team.
- Consult with and support the leadership and activism of communities facing institutional barriers.
- Engage in conversations around race and social justice issues on an ongoing basis.
- Infuse cultural relevance in all professional development and ask questions when it is not there.

Adapted from Katz 1978.

# Appendix E

## Definitions

When engaging in dialogue about race, many people struggle with finding the right words to share their thoughts. We provided the following list to help you better understand what we mean when referencing different terms in this book. We encourage you to research and explore beyond these short definitions to help you navigate conversations on race.

### Culture
The language, traditions, history, and ancestry people have in common. People that share a common culture are "ethnic" groups. All people have culture; it is fluid and dynamic.

### Discrimination
Unequal treatment of a person based on their membership in a group. In contrast to prejudice, discrimination is behavior.

### Dominant Culture
Common beliefs, values, and behaviors of privileged groups (white, male, heterosexual, cis-gender, wealthy, etc.) that usually go unnamed and are considered the "norm" against which others are measured.

### Equality
"In any given circumstances, people who are the same in those respects relevant to how they are treated in those circumstances should receive the same treatment" (45). Equality defined in this way, looks at the individual and the circumstances surrounding him or her. It does not focus on group differences based on categories, such as race, sex, social class, and ethnicity. This view is one of assimilation because it assumes that individuals, once socialized into society, have the right "to do anything they want, to choose their own lives and not be hampered by traditional expectations and stereotypes" (Young 1990, 157).

### Equity
According to Krause, Traini, and Mickey (2001), equity "deals with difference and takes into consideration the fact that this society has many groups in it who have not always been given equal treatment and/or have not had a level field on which to play. These groups have been frequently made to feel inferior to those in the mainstream, and some have been oppressed. . . .

Thus, the concept of equity provides a case for unequal treatment for those who have been disadvantaged over time. It can provide compensatory kinds of treatment, offering it in the form of special programs and benefits for those who have been discriminated against and are in need of opportunity" (76–90).

### Ethnicity
A social construction that indicates identification with a particular group that is often descended from common ancestors. Members of the group share common cultural traits, such as language, religion, and dress.

### Institutional Racism
The network of institutional structures, policies, and practices that create advantages and benefits for whites, and discrimination, oppression, and disadvantages for people from targeted racial groups.

### Internalized Oppression
When members of a target group believe, act on, or enforce the dominant system of beliefs about themselves and members of their own group. For example, internalized sexism involves women applying principles of male dominance and oppression to themselves and/or other women.

### Internalized Superiority
When members of an agent group accept their group's socially and politically superior status as normal and deserved. For example, internalized white superiority is the belief and actions based on the idea that white people are superior.

### Intersectionality
An approach largely advanced by women of color, arguing that classifications such as gender, race, class, and others cannot be examined in isolation from one another; they interact and intersect in individuals' lives, in society, in social systems, and are mutually constitutive.

### Nationality
One's country of origin or citizenship.

### Oppression
Systemic devaluing, undermining, marginalizing, and disadvantaging of certain social identities in contrast to the privileged norm; when some people are denied something of value, while others have ready access.

### People of Color (POC)
A term born out of the antiracism movement used to describe nonwhites. The term is meant to be inclusive among nonwhite groups, emphasizing common experiences of racism and oppression and resistance against it.

### Privilege
Systemic favoring, enriching, valuing, validating, and including of certain social identities over others. Individuals cannot "opt out" of systems of privilege; these systems are inherent to the society in which we live.

## Race

There is no biological basis for racial categories, and genetic research has shown we have more within-group variation than between-group variations. Races are socially and politically constructed categories that others have assigned on the basis of physical characteristics, such as skin color or hair type. Although there are no races, perceptions of race influence our beliefs, stereotypes, economic opportunities, and everyday experiences.

## Racial/Ethnic Identity

Racial/ethnic identity development is a sense of self that is shaped over time by experiences. Because we live in a society that stereotypes groups of people, most often people of color, in negative ways it is important to have a foundational strength rooted in who you are that is able to effectively deal with society's -isms. There is research that shows the more you see your racial/ethnic identity in positive ways and take pride in your group identity, the more positive your mental health. Racial/ethnic identity develops over time. It is not linear but rather circular, meaning that people can go in and out of stages of development, returning to an old way of thinking or remaining in one particular stage for a long period of time.

## Racism

Institutional power and prejudice against subordinated members of targeted racial groups (Blacks, Latin@s, Native Americans, Asians) by members of the agent racial group (whites). This happens at the individual, cultural, and institutional level. Racism can involve both conscious, intentional action and unconscious or unintentional collusion.

## Stereotype

An overgeneralization based on race, gender, sexual orientation, class, ability, age, and other characteristics that is widely believed about an entire group of people. Stereotypes are impervious to evidence and contrary argument.

## White Privilege

A system of unearned benefits afforded to those people classified as white. These advantages are personal, cultural, and institutional and provide greater access to resources and systemic power. For white people, white privilege leads to a form of internalized oppression as it distorts their relationships and humanity.

## White Supremacy Culture

The systemic dominance of white culture based on the assumption or theory that whites are inherently superior to all other races and should be in power and control.

*Definitions adapted from:*

The People's Institute NW, http://pinwseattle.org/.
Copyright © 2014 White Privilege Conference, www.whiteprivilegeconference.com.
Wijeysinghe, C. L., Griffin, P., and Love, B. (1997). "Racism Curriculum Design." In M. Adams, L. A. Bell, and P. Griffin (eds.), *Teaching for Diversity and Social Justice: A Sourcebook* (pp. 82–109). New York: Routledge.

# Appendix F

## Sample Agenda

| Time | Notes | What's Needed | Learning Objectives |
|---|---|---|---|
| 8:00–8:30 (30 min) | SETTING THE STAGE<br>Introduction of facilitator(s)<br>Purpose & Objectives<br>Norms<br>Question/Comments | Norm Cards<br>3 x 5 cards | Develop connection between facilitator and presenter. Clear understanding of objectives for the day. |
| 8:30–8:55 (25 min) | REFLECTION<br>Think-Pair-Share: When did you first realize that race mattered? | Journals | Tap into prior experiences. We all notice race. |
| 8:55–9:55 (60 min) | DEFINING CULTURAL COMPETENCE<br>Write responses on poster paper<br>Build on their knowledge, then show PowerPoint<br>Pair-Share: How does this connect to your work? | Poster Paper<br>Markers<br>Cultural Competence Handout | Develop understanding and framework for cultural competence |
| Break 9:55–10:10 (15 min) | | | |
| 10:10–12:10 (2 hours) | STEREOTYPE/LABELING ACTIVITY<br>In your groups list stereotypes (7 min)<br>Discuss impact of stereotypes (10 min)<br>20/20 Video<br>Large Group Discussion | Poster Paper<br>Markers<br>Video | Increase understanding of the impact of stereotypes. |
| Lunch 12:10–1:10 (1 hour) | | | |
| 1:10–2:40 (90 min) | COLOR LINE<br>Complete survey<br>Line up against wall<br>Large group discussion | Survey<br>3 x 5 cards on wall | Develop understanding of unearned privileges and the impact on marginalized groups |
| Break 2:40–2:50 (10 min) | | | |
| 2:50–3:10 20 min | THINK-PAIR-SHARE/LARGE GROUP<br>One thing you learned<br>One thing you will try differently as a result of what you learned<br>One question you still have<br>Large group discussion | Journal | Reflect on the day |
| 3:10–3:30 20 min | CLOSING<br>Questions/Comments<br>Read Poem<br>Evaluations/Clock Hours | Evaluations<br>Clock Hour Forms | |

# Appendix G

## Sample Workshop Evaluation Form

Organization: _____    Date: _____
Title of Presentation: _____
Presenter(s): _____

Please circle the number that corresponds to how much you agree with the following statements:

ABOUT THE PRESENTER(S)
**1. The presenter(s) clearly communicated the subject matter.**

| 6 | 5 | 4 | 3 | 2 | 1 |
|---|---|---|---|---|---|
| Strongly Agree | Agree | Mildly Agree | Mildly Disagree | Disagree | Strongly Disagree |

**2. The presenter(s) were skillful in facilitating discussions and activities.**

| 6 | 5 | 4 | 3 | 2 | 1 |
|---|---|---|---|---|---|
| Strongly Agree | Agree | Mildly Agree | Mildly Disagree | Disagree | Strongly Disagree |

**3. To the extent that circumstances permitted, the presenter(s) encouraged interaction among participants and allowed time for questions and answers.**

| 6 | 5 | 4 | 3 | 2 | 1 |
|---|---|---|---|---|---|
| Strongly Agree | Agree | Mildly Agree | Mildly Disagree | Disagree | Strongly Disagree |

CONTENT OF PRESENTATION
**4. Discussion, exercises, and presentations stimulated me to think about the subject matter to a greater extent than I had before participating in this workshop.**

| 6 | 5 | 4 | 3 | 2 | 1 |
|---|---|---|---|---|---|
| Strongly Agree | Agree | Mildly Agree | Mildly Disagree | Disagree | Strongly Disagree |

**5. The workshop was well organized and activities clearly emphasized major points.**

| 6 | 5 | 4 | 3 | 2 | 1 |
|---|---|---|---|---|---|
| Strongly Agree | Agree | Mildly Agree | Mildly Disagree | Disagree | Strongly Disagree |

**6. The content of the workshop enhanced my overall understanding of the topic.**

| 6 | 5 | 4 | 3 | 2 | 1 |
|---|---|---|---|---|---|
| Strongly Agree | Agree | Mildly Agree | Mildly Disagree | Disagree | Strongly Disagree |

**7. The materials provided were helpful.**

| 6 | 5 | 4 | 3 | 2 | 1 |
|---|---|---|---|---|---|
| Strongly Agree | Agree | Mildly Agree | Mildly Disagree | Disagree | Strongly Disagree |

COMMENTS

8. What aspects of this workshop contributed the <u>most</u> to your learning?

_____

_____

9. How could this workshop be improved?

_____

_____

10. Is culturally relevant professional development (CRPD) something you feel should be ongoing in your organization? Please explain.

_____

_____

11. What other culturally relevant professional development (CRPD) would you like to participate in?

_____

_____

12. What is one thing you will do differently or one strategy you will try, as a result of what you learned today?

_____

_____

13. Any thoughts or comments you have about the presenter(s) skill, style, etc.?

_____

_____

   How did you hear about this workshop?
☐ Friend ☐ I'm on your mailing list ☐ Conference ☐ Website ☐ Other _____

Thank you for your participation and feedback!

# Acknowledgments

I would first like to give thanks and honor to God for blessing me with experiences and challenges that I didn't always appreciate or welcome at the time but now realize contributed to my personal and professional growth. I know in my heart that who I am today and everything I have in my life is because of Him and for that I'm truly grateful. Where would I be without my mother, Darlene Jones, a strong woman, who early on planted seeds of social justice in my heart and soul, modeled what it means to truly love another human being unconditionally, and taught me the true meaning of family? Thanks to my dad, Sam Jones, who taught me it is never too late to establish meaningful relationships. To my grandparents, Marion and George Simmons, who loved me well; my grandfather never learned to read and write but always showed me the difference between right and wrong. I miss you.

A special thanks to my husband, Gary Hollins, who was always patient, for believing I could do it, whatever "it" was, and for being proud of me and my accomplishments. I'm proud of you, too. To my siblings, Mike, Ted, Mark, Kelly, Suzanne (Suki), Robert, and Judy, whom I have fought with, cried with, loved and grew with, to you I say, "Ubuntu (I am because we are)." A very special thanks to my business partner and coauthor, Ilsa Govan. What can I say, partner, you rock! I'm quite blessed to have you as a colleague in this difficult and challenging venture. To Dr. Jennifer Wiley, a wonderful friend and supporter, who is always there pushing me to grow in my understanding of social justice, challenging me to think more deeply about complex issues, and knows what it means to be a true friend. Thank you Pat Siggs, Joan Trunk, and Diane Huey for always cheering me on and supporting me through tough times. You have made a difference in my life, and I thank you for everything you have done for me. I want to thank my stepchildren, Jovan, Akilah, and Marques Hollins, who throughout the years have taught me that relationships can be a lot of work but the outcome is well worth the time and energy invested.

A special thanks to many of my former students, who have been instrumental in my growth as a teacher, and also to those who have ever attended one of my workshops—most of what is in this book comes from what I have learned from you.

This work is challenging and demanding but with all of the support I've had over the years, how could I not be successful? Thank you. I am truly blessed to have you in my life.

—Caprice Hollins

I am grateful to my family for the countless times you've talked, listened, and learned along with me. To my dad, who has shown me what it really means to take risks. To my mom and Jeff, who attended my first keynote lecture, make me amazing dinners after presentations, and are constantly reading, watching videos, and having conversations about stuff that matters. Mom, I'm your biggest fan. To Alexis, who models the power of humor as a tool for education. I love it when we laugh so hard no one else understands us. Thank you, Paul, for listening and talking me down after a long, not necessarily hard, day. I also want to recognize The Team. I'll take one for you any time.

I want to thank my amazing business partner, Caprice Hollins, without whose dreams and dedication Cultures Connecting and this book would not exist. I deeply value our conversations about who we are, what we're doing, and how we improve and grow together. Thank you for your willingness to bring up the hard stuff and mentoring me in sharing my own vulnerabilities.

Thank you to all of the people who have trusted me enough to share your stories. Thank you to my antiracist allies, especially the members of WEACT, who have cared enough to offer me critical feedback. I will never forget the Women's Center staff at WWU who first suggested we watch *The Color of Fear* together. And, finally, I'd like to recognize the educators and students at Pacific Oaks Northwest, an incredible learning institution that pushed me to new depths of understanding.

—Ilsa M. Govan

# References

Atkinson, D. R., Morten, G., and Sue, D. W., eds. (1993). *Counseling American minorities: A cross-cultural perspective* (4th ed.). Dubuque, IA: William C. Brown.

Christensen, L. (2000). *Reading, writing, and rising up: Teaching about social justice and the power of the written word*. Milwaukee: A Rethinking Schools Publication.

*The Color of Fear* (1994). Directed by Lee Mun Wah.

Dillard, A. (1982). *Teaching a stone to talk*. New York: HarperCollins.

Katz, J. H. (1978). *White awareness: Handbook for anti-racism training*. Norman: University of Oklahoma Press.

Krause, J. K., Traini. D. J., and Mickey, B. H. (2001). *Equality versus equity*. In J. P. Shapiro and J. A. Stefkovick (eds.), *Ethical leadership and decision making in education* (76–90). Mahwah, NJ: Lawrence Erlbaum.

Obear, K. (2007). "Navigating triggering events: Critical skills for facilitating difficult dialogue." *The Diversity Factor* 15, no. 3. http://drkathyobear.files.wordpress.com/2013/04/navigating-triggering-events.pdf.

Palmer, P. J. (2000). *Let your life speak: Listening for the voice of vocation*. San Francisco: Jossey-Bass.

Public Conversations Project (2011). *Constructive conversations about challenging times: A guide to community dialogue*. Watertown, MA: www.publicconversations.org.

Singleton, G. E., and Linton, C. (2006). *Courageous conversations about race: A field guide for achieving equity in schools*. Thousand Oaks, CA: Corwin.

Steele, C. M. (2010). *Whistling Vivaldi. And other clues to how stereotypes affect us*. New York: Norton.

Stone, D., Patton, B., and Heen, S. (1999). *Difficult conversations: How to discuss what matters most*. New York: Penguin.

Sue, D. W., Capodilupo, C. M., Torino, G. C., Bucceri, J., Holder, A. M. B., Nadal, K. L., and Esquilin, M. (2007). *Racial microaggressions in everyday life: Implications for clinical practice. American Psychologist* 62, no. 4, 271–86.

Sue, D. W., and Sue, D. (2003). *Counseling the culturally diverse: Theory and practice* (4th ed.). New York: John Wiley.

Sue, D. W., and Sue, D., eds. (2013). *Counseling the culturally diverse: Theory and practice*. Hoboken, NJ: Wiley & Sons.

Wile, Daniel B. (2009). *Collaborative couples therapy: Turning fights into intimate conversations. R. Cassidy Seminars*. June 2009.

Young, I. M. (1990). *Justice and the politics of difference*. Princeton: Princeton University Press.

# Recommended Resources

Almost everything you do will seem insignificant. But it is very important that you do it …
You must be the change you wish to see in the world.

—Mahatma Gandhi

## BOOKS AND ARTICLES ON FACILITATING

Bolgatz, J. (2005). *Talking race in the classroom*. New York: Teacher College Press.

Grineski, S., Landsman, J., and Simmons, R. (2013). *Talking about race: Alleviating the fear*. Sterling, VA: Stylus.

Mindell, A. (1995). *Sitting in the fire: Large group transformation using conflict and diversity*. Portland, OR: Lao Tse.

Norris, J. A., (2003). *From telling to teaching: A dialogue approach to adult learning*. North Myrtle Beach, SC: Learning by Dialogue Publishing.

Parker, R., and Smith Chambers, P. (2005). *The anti-racist cookbook: A recipe guide for conversations about race that goes beyond covered dishes and "Kum-Bah-Ya."* Roselle, NJ: Crandall, Dostie & Douglass.

Proudford, K. (2002) *Asking the question: Uncovering the assumptions that undermine conversations across race*. Simmons School of Management; CGO Insights. http://www.simmons.edu/som/docs/Insights_14.pdf.

Stephens, V. M. (2006) *Moving past the silence: A tool for negotiating reflective conversations about race: Moving philanthropy closer to racial equality and social justice*. Minneapolis: Effective Communities. http://www.effectivecommunities.com/pdfs/ECP_ReflectiveConversations.pdf.

## BOOKS AND ARTICLES FOR DEEPENING YOUR UNDERSTANDING OF RACISM AND PRIVILEGE

Atkinson, D. R., Morten, G., and Sue, D. W., eds. (1993). *Counseling American minorities: A cross-cultural perspective* (4th ed.). Dubuque, IA: William C. Brown

166

Barndt, J. (2007). *Understanding and dismantling racism: The twenty-first century challenge to white America*. Minneapolis: Fortress.

Bell, D. (1992). *Faces at the bottom of the well*. New York: Basic Books.

Carlos Poston, W. S. (1990). "The biracial identity development model: A needed addition." *Journal of Counseling & Development* 69, 152–55.

Cross, W. E. (1971). "The Negro-to-Black conversion experience: Toward a psychology of Black liberation." *Black World* 20, 13–27.

Degruy Leary, J. (2005). *Post-traumatic slave syndrome: America's legacy of enduring injury and healing*. Milwaukee; Uptone.

Freire, P. (2000). *Pedagogy of the oppressed: 30th anniversary edition*. London: Continuum.

Kendall, F. E. (2013). *Understanding white privilege: Creating pathways to authentic relationships across race* (2nd ed.). New York: Routledge.

Kim, J. (1981). *Process of Asian-American identity development: A study of Japanese American women's perceptions of their struggle to achieve positive identities*. PhD dissertation, University of Massachusetts.

Kivel, P. (2002). *Uprooting racism: How white people can work for racial justice* (2nd ed.). Gabriola Island, BC: New Society.

Lipsitz, G. (1998). *The possessive investment in whiteness: How white people benefit from identity politics*. Philadelphia: Temple University Press.

McGoldrick, M., Giordano, J., and Pearce, J. K., eds. (1996). *Ethnicity and family therapy* (2nd ed.). New York: Guilford.

McIntosh, P. (1998). *White privilege and male privilege: A personal account of coming to see correspondences through work in women studies*. Working paper no. 189. Wellesley College, Wellesley, MA.

Norris, J. A. (2003). *From telling to teaching: A dialogue approach to adult learning*. North Myrtle Beach, SC: Learning by Dialogue Publishing.

Palmer, P. J. (2011). *Healing the heart of democracy: The courage to create a politics worthy of the human spirit*. San Francisco: Jossey-Bass.

Ponterotto, J. G., and Pedersen, P. B. (1993). *Preventing prejudice: A guide for counselors and educators*. Newbury Park, CA: Sage.

Rogat Loeb, P. (1999). *Soul of a citizen: Living with conviction in a cynical time*. New York: St. Martin's Griffin.

Ruiz, A. S. (1990). "Ethnic identity: Crisis and resolution." *Journal of Multicultural Counseling and Development* 24, 161–87.

Steele, Claude (2010). *Whistling Vivaldi: And other clues to how stereotypes affect us*. New York: W. W. Norton.

Stone, D., Patton, B., and Heen, S. (1999). *Difficult conversations: How to discuss what matters most*. New York: Penguin.

Takaki, R. (1993). *A different mirror: A history of multicultural America*. Boston: Little, Brown.

Tatum, B. D. (1997). *Why are all the black kids sitting together in the cafeteria: And other conversations about race*. New York: Basic Books.

Van Ausdale, D., and Feagin, J. (2001) *The first R: How children learn race and racism*. New York: Rowman and Littlefield.

## DVDS/VIDEOS

*Ethnic Notions*, by Marlon Riggs—56 minutes (1987).

*The Color of Fear*, by Lee Mun Wah—90 minutes (1995). Stir Fry Seminars & Consulting

*Last Chance for Eden*, by Lee Mun Wah (2002). Stir Fry Seminars & Consulting

*The Shadow of Hate: A History of Intolerance in America*, by Charles Guggenheim—40 minutes (1995).

*Unnatural Causes: Is Inequality Making Us Sick* • 7 segments—4 hours total (2008).

*Mirrors of Privilege: Making Whiteness Visible*, by Shakti Butler—50 minutes.

*Race the Power of an Illusion*, by California Newsreel · 3 episodes—56 minutes each (2003).

*How to Tell People They Sound Racist*, by Jay Smooth—3 minutes (2008). http://www.illdoctrine. com/2008/07/how_to_tell_people_they_sound.html.


## WEBSITES

www.arc.org/—The Applied Research Center is a public policy, educational and research institute whose work emphasizes issues of race and social change.

http://www.arabfilm.com/item/220/—*In My Own Skin: The Complexity of Living as an Arab in American*. Video clips and information pertaining to the Arab Culture and Civilization.

www.asian-nation.org/assimilation.shtml—Asian Nation: Asian American History, Demographics, & Issues.

http://www.crr.ca/en/programs/35-youth/21690-the-kit-a-manual-by-youth-to-combat-racism-through-education—"The KIT" is a bilingual manual containing 61 pages of information, history, resources, and tools for anti-racism education.

www.densho.org—Densho: The Japanese American Legacy Project.

www.diversitycentral.com—Conferences, shopping, articles, employment, celebrations and more.

https://implicit.harvard.edu/implicit/—Tests for unconscious bias for race, age, gender, sexual orientation, and body image.

www.mavinfoundation.org/projects/magazine.html—MAVIN Foundation: The Mixed Race Experience.

www.racialequitytools.org—Designed to support individuals and groups working to achieve racial equity.

www.racialicious.com—Blog about race and pop culture.

www.reducingstereotypethreat.org—A wealth of information on what is stereotype threat, the consequences, situations that lead to it, what can be done to reduce it, etc.

www.rethinkingschools.org—Rethinking Schools is a nonprofit publisher and advocacy organization dedicated to sustaining and strengthening public education through social justice teaching and education activism.

www.teachingtolerance.org—Resources for children, teens, parents, and teachers on valuing diversity.

www.thesocietypages.org/socimages/—Sociological Images provides keen media analysis for sharpening your lens around issues of oppression.

# About the Authors

**Caprice Hollins** received her doctorate degree in clinical psychology with an emphasis in multicultural and community psychology from California School of Professional Psychology–Los Angeles. She is an assistant professor of counseling at the Seattle School of Theology & Psychology and cofounder of Cultures Connecting.

**Ilsa Govan,** cofounder of Cultures Connecting, is deeply invested in understanding how privilege, power, and culture influence our lives in order to advocate for equity and justice. She has a master's degree in bicultural human development from Pacific Oaks College and a K–12 teaching certificate in special education and English language learning.